The Student Fundraising Handbook

Never shake your bucket, and everything else you need to know

Sarah Hewett

studentfundraisinghandbook.org

Acknowledgements

My thanks go to all the people who have shown an interest and given me support in the process of writing this book; also to everyone who made fundraising such great fun when I was a student. To name a few:

Fran for suggesting Charities Rep roles and for having me to stay when I arrived in London. James, Jono, Louise and Lils for being great and for keeping me mad.

The Oxford RAG committee for being fearless, ambitious and great friends (as well as for the quotes).

Will for the friendship, food and reverse psychology.

Rebekah for the words of wisdom and our trip to pat-a-pain.

Everyone at Student Hubs for living the values which this book represents and proving what our generation are capable of. Graham for the brilliant cover design and enthusiasm for the idea.

Maria for unwavering confidence in the idea.

Raja for being an inspiration and not minding that I quit.

Tom for being wonderful. I owe you a lot of washing up.

My lovely Mum, Dad and sister Gemma for their constant support despite my seemingly mad ideas and for never taking me too seriously (as well as for the legal advice). My cousin James for his experience and quotes.

Emily, Sophie and Amelia - I'm lucky to have a bunch of friends as bright and eclectic as you.

Innocent Drinks (and all the lovely friends who work there) for their generous scholarship which has allowed me to get this book published.

This book is dedicated to young people. Believe in your ability to make the world a better place.

Author's Biography

Sarah is an Oxford University graduate with substantial experience in student-level fundraising for charities and good causes:

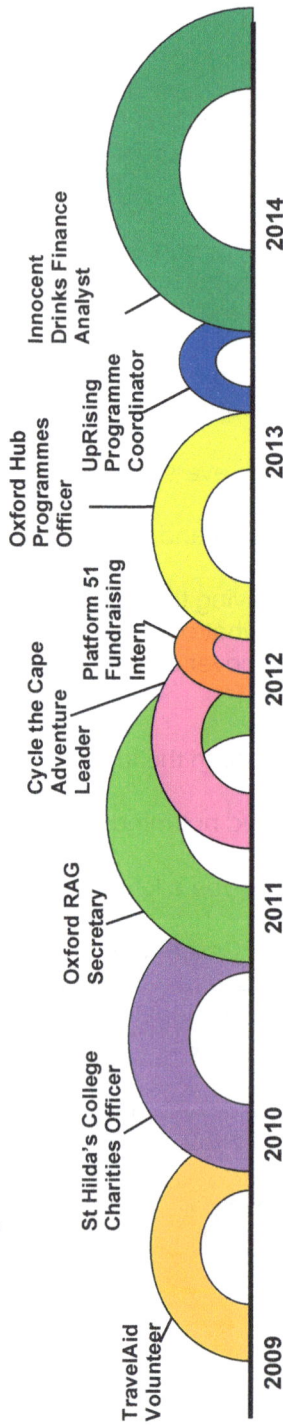

TravelAid Volunteer — 2009

St Hilda's College Charities Officer — 2010

Oxford RAG Secretary — 2011

Cycle the Cape Adventure Leader

Platform 51 Fundraising Intern — 2012

Oxford Hub Programmes Officer

UpRising Programme Coordinator — 2013

Innocent Drinks Finance Analyst — 2014

In the name of fundraising, she has organised conferences for over 800 young people, raised over £50,000 for more than 50 good causes, she has gone without shoes for a week, tied herself to a friend for a week and organised many of the ideas listed in this book.

She is writing this book in response to a gap in available comprehensive resources for young people at all stages of involvement n fundraising activities.

The Student Fundraising Handbook

Contents

Introduction

Fundraising is both great fun and incredibly important to support good causes, however big or small. Whatever your experience, this book will help you to be more effective, be more creative and ultimately raise more money.

Students are some of the most passionate and active people in the world and possess the great resources of creativity, flexibility and networks of friends and contacts. Students have been making use of these resources for generations to raise funds for fantastic causes and make a really positive difference in the world. Student fundraisers are also incredibly diverse and interesting, raising for causes from better recycling facilities in a school to supporting local hospices, taking part in 10k challenges for national charities to volunteering projects across the world. More and more causes are recognising how valuable students can be as a unique group of fundraisers and supporters. This book will support you whether you're planning a stall at a school fair or running a university fundraising group.

The book offers advice on how to get started in fundraising, behind-the-scenes skills to make the most out of any fundraising opportunity, step-by-step guides for a huge variety of fundraising initiatives and sample documents you can apply to your own cause.

As well as the good advice, the book offers plenty of first-hand case studies, tips and tricks to make your job easier and what not to do in fundraising, and focuses on some of the bigger questions you're bound to be asked or ask yourself while fundraising.

All of this comes from young people who have been there and done it all themselves!

What is Fundraising?

Fundraising is as simple as it sounds: it's raising money. In this book, it's raising money for a good cause.

It's widely believed that effective fundraising is entrepreneurial, social and enjoyable. It can also educate and engage people about important issues, but should not focus on negative emotions around these issues to coerce people into donating.

Student fundraising has always been based on giving people a good time and something in return; it's much more than shaking buckets (or, as the subtitle suggests, refraining from shaking your bucket)! This might be getting a chocolate brownie at a cake sale or it might mean the experience of doing a bungee jump and being sponsored for a good cause. Some of the earliest university RAG (Raise and Give) groups used to sell joke books called 'RAG mags' to raise funds.

The aim of this book is to make sure you understand how good causes operate, to make fundraising accessible and fun and to help you develop as a person while you're doing it. With this resource to guide you, you can avoid mistakes which have been made before and focus on fundraising really effectively.

Why Fundraise?

You might be interested in fundraising for a huge number of reasons. Each person's motivation is very different, but some popular reasons are:

"This cause means a lot to me" Many people choose to fundraise after they have been personally supported by a cause, maybe a family member was cared for in a hospital or the football club you were part of has fallen on hard times. This sort of authentic personal link means you will really know the cause and people will take your fundraising more seriously.

"It gives me something more interesting to do" While your friends are panicking about assignments or watching cats play the piano on YouTube, you're out running incredible events, telling people about a cause you're really passionate about and seeing the world. Then, next time your Gran asks what you do with your time, you'll have plenty to say!

"I want to make a difference" A lot of students choose to fundraise because they know how lucky they are and want to give others the same opportunity. This is great, but remember to do some research about exactly where the money you raise goes so you can explain what the difference you're making is. See page 12 for more details on knowing your cause.

"It's great fun" It really is! Fundraising is a fantastic way to make friends, to experience things you wouldn't get to do otherwise, to be silly, wear fancy dress at 10 in the morning and to count up money by the bucketful.

"It looks great to employers" This is very true: showing you have an interest in good causes and the skills to raise amounts of money is very impressive to employers and will make you more creative, organised and interesting to talk to. Some people begin fundraising for this reason, but almost always continue to fundraise because of the friends they make, the fun they have and the compassion they develop for the cause. For more resources on employability, see pages 108 to 109 in the Resources section.

Tom Fraine, Talent Team Leader at Innocent Drinks recommends fundraising as a way to impress an employer:

"At innocent we look for people who are the right fit, which means they need to be great at doing the job but we also want them to be interesting, entrepreneurial and generous people. Fundraising experience can show that a person has a broad range of skills, has worked with a range of different stakeholders and will know about making a profit – in the same way businesses need to. As Innocent gives 10% of profits to charity, it also shows they fit with our values."

How To Get Started

Know Your Cause

Before setting out on any fundraising initiative, you need to know your cause and know where the money you raise will go.

Smaller causes are often easier to explain than big ones: funding a new football kit for your old team so they can compete can't raise too many questions but raising for bigger organisations to alleviate famine or to help prevent climate change can be much more complicated. If you can answer questions about your cause with confidence and authority, you will be taken more seriously and are likely to raise more money. Here are some questions you might be asked and how to find the answers:

What is a charity?

In the UK, a charity is an organisation registered with the Charities Commission. They are the regulator of charities and aim to "increase charities' efficiency and effectiveness and public trust in them". However, not all good causes (often seen as charities) are registered, and not all registered charities are in need of fundraisers. For example, many very small causes are not registered because they can't be if they raise less than £5,000 per year and it takes time and resources to apply for registration which they could use for better things. Interestingly, some purely political oganisations are not allowed to register, as their aims do not qualify as being fully charitable. Therefore Amnesty International, to take one example, is not a charity. On the other hand, independent schools can register, so some of the most elite academic institutions in the country are officially charities.

Is my cause a charity?

You can easily check by asking whether they're registered and therefore if they have a charity number. Using the Charity Commission website, you can search by their name or by the charity number to see a host of information about their performance. If your cause could qualify as a charity and isn't already registered, you may be able to look into getting it registered as a charity here: https://www.gov.uk/setting-up-charity. If you're not raising for a charity, ask why the cause doesn't qualify so you can explain that, as well as the good work they do, to others.

What do they do?

Most organisations will have a clear mission, often reflected in their name and slogan: NSPCC work to stop cruelty to children, Friends of the Earth want to protect the planet. You should be able to explain in a sentence what your cause does, but also to expand on that for people who are more interested, with examples and statistics. If you don't already know these, ask someone within the cause (all large charities have a full-time fundraising department who will be happy to talk to you) or do some research on their website. For example

> "The NSPCC has over 40 service centres across the UK where we work face to face with children, young people and families who need our help." (NSPCC Website, January 2012)

Does all the money go to the cause?

If you're raising to make a direct donation, the answer will be yes. Remember, some of the donation may go towards admin costs like paying staff and for offices, and all charities must be able to give you a break-down of how their income is spent. There is no right and wrong answer about how much goes on things like salaries, overheads and administrative costs, as all charities work differently, but the charity must be able to justify what they spend their money on. Jessica Wiliams, author of How to Give to Charity says:

"If a charity spends very little on fundraising, salaries and administration, that may not actually be a good thing: it may mean that it's not investing enough in its own infrastructure and it isn't paying competitive salaries to attract the best people. Both of these factors will affect the charity's ability to achieve its long-term goals. But on the other hand, administration costs have to be kept under control."

Oxfam are one of the best-known charities in the UK. Here is how their spending breaks down:

For every £1 donated to Oxfam...

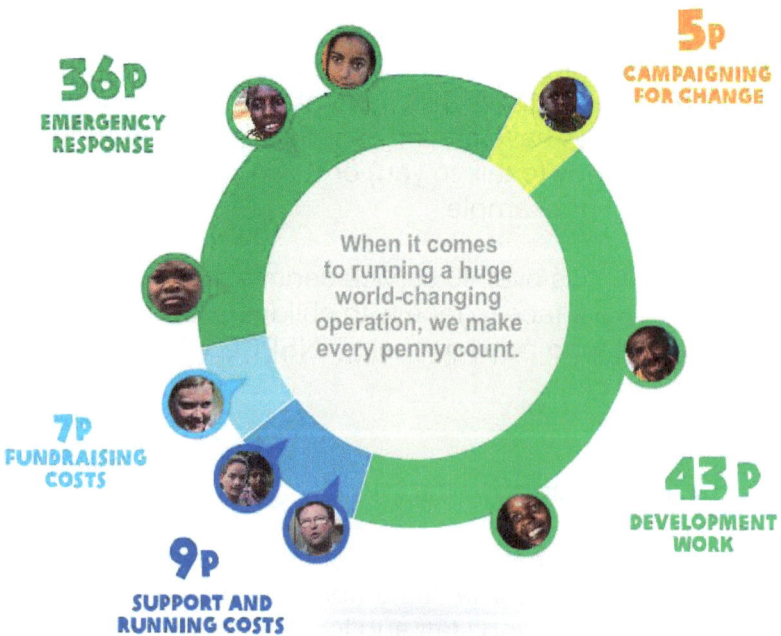

36P
EMERGENCY RESPONSE

5p
CAMPAIGNING FOR CHANGE

When it comes to running a huge world-changing operation, we make every penny count.

7P
FUNDRAISING COSTS

9P
SUPPORT AND RUNNING COSTS

43 P
DEVELOPMENT WORK

Oxfam say this:

"At Oxfam, we work hard to make sure we keep our costs to a minimum and the donations we receive are used in the most effective and responsible way. I hope it will reassure you to know that, on average, for every £1 donated to Oxfam's general funds, 84p is spent on emergency, development and campaigning work, 9p is spent on support and governance and 7p is invested to generate future income.

Like all charities in England and Wales, Oxfam is regulated by the Charity Commission (www.charity-commission.gov.uk), which is responsible for ensuring that all our funds are being used correctly. Our accounts are audited, approved and submitted to the Charity Commission every year." (email correspondence, 2014)

Is it OK if some of my fundraising goes to pay for me?

In cases where you're raising for a challenge event (like a 10K run or volunteering overseas) some of the money may go to the cause initially but then be spent by them on your expenses, like a participant's T-shirt, entry fee and even flights and accommodation for international challenges or projects. Make sure you know what the case is with your cause, know the figures and be honest with anyone who asks.

Where will the money be spent?

With larger organisations, people may be interested in whether the money is spent at home (in the UK) or abroad, or whether money is given to individuals or to governments or other groups. You should be able to get all of this information from someone from within the cause.

If you can't find the answers to any of these questions, stop fundraising and keep asking until you're satisfied.

But I'm not raising for a charity. Is this book for me?

It's alright to raise money for things like expeditions and things which will benefit you, and this book will definitely help! However, it's important that you are always honest with the people who are donating that you are not raising for charity and you can be clear about how their money will be spent. There may also be certain ideas which won't work as well for you, for example, sponsorship from phil- anthropic causes and street collections. However, take a look at page 82 (Challenge Event) if you're raising for an expedition.

Fundraising Vocab

We're going to get a bit geeky about this, so if you're not sure of the difference between a RAG Raid and an assault on a carpet shop (RAG/rug, geddit?!) then here's your chance to swot up!

Challenge Event

Whether running a 10K at home or climbing Mount Kilimanjaro or Machu Picchu, there are loads of opportunities for students to do these sorts of challenges for good causes. People are often sponsored for the challenge, but some have bigger demands on fundraising, so you may have to run other initiatives to raise funds prior to the event itself. On page 82 (challenge Event) there is a fundraising breakdown you can use in preparation for a marathon or similar challenge.

Donor

A donor is someone who gives money to the good cause. A lot of charities work on engaging donors who have given once but may be interested in doing so again if there is a good event or opportunity for them. The Know Your Audience pages (page 20) will help you to think about your donors and how to make them happy and interested.

GiftAid

This is a way for people to claim back income tax (which is automatically deducted at 20% - correct in 2014 - by the UK government when your salary exceeds the tax-free allowance) on charitable donations. This means that a donation of £10 goes to the charity as £12.50, as the tax has been replaced on it. It can be time-consuming and fiddly to sort out GiftAid for small donations, so we don't think it's necessary for most of the initiatives in this book, but if you're getting serious, talk to any organisation you're raising for or do more research online.

Philanthropy

The basis behind a lot of charitable organisations lies in the old idea of philanthropy. During the Industrial Revolution, it became popular for owners of industry to invest in libraries, schools and hospitals for their local communities (often made up of the workers from their factories). This led to the creation of a lot of charities who still rely on donations from the public, such as the charity Barnardo's.

RAG Group

Many universities and some schools and colleges have societies dedicated to fundraising. Names can vary but a popular one is RAG, originally from 'Raise and Give'. RAG groups in the UK are growing rapidly and gather annually for a RAG Conference. More details on the conference can be found in the Useful Links section (page 111).

Raid

In order to increase the intrigue and excitement around street collections, they've been re-branded as 'Raids'. Depending on who organises the event, they can involve a coach ride to another city for a day with drinks and food on the way home and sometimes prizes for the people who have collected the most.

In-kind Donations

These are donations of things which are not money but can still help in your fundraising efforts. It could be a voucher for a meal in a restaurant which can be the prize in a raffle or a day of training for your committee which makes you better public speakers about the cause. It's well worth approaching some places specifically for in-kind donations instead of money, especially businesses, as they are more likely to give and it plays to everyone's strengths.

Piggybacking

When you run an event which is part of someone else's event, like a stall at a car boot sale or a barbecue at a sports event. It means someone else has done the hard work to bring lots of people to one place and you can offer a service and profit from it. This is a great first step when you're new to fundraising!

Know your Audience

When fundraising, different strategies and approaches work with different groups of people. The people you can work with for fundraising can be divided into three groups:

Friends and Family
Your nearest and dearest.

Good things
They are likely to support you because they know and respect you as an individual. They may offer time and resources (like space to hold events or baking skills) as well as or instead of money. They will probably be happy to tell loads of other people about what you're doing, too!

Bad Things
If you approach them in the wrong way, you could cause lasting damage to your most important relationships.

Best Fundraising Ideas
Christmas Cards (page 53), Clothes Swap (page 38).

Organisations and Groups
These range from groups you know personally, such as sports clubs, church groups or your school up to much larger organisations such as your university, philanthropic clubs and even businesses.

Good Things
Groups provide a way of reaching far more people with your cause and create a network for publicity for events.

Bad Things
Each group should be approached individually and many will not be interested in supporting you, so it can be very time-consuming.

Best Fundraising Ideas
Corporate Sponsorship (page 68), Organise a Challenge Event (page 100).

Everyone Else
This really does mean everyone else!

Good Things
The people are endless, giving can be quick and having a big smile on your face, sincere knowledge of your cause and lots of energy can make all the difference.

Bad Things
These people don't have any prior interest in you or your cause, so the majority will just ignore you.

Best Fundraising Ideas
Street Collections (page 66), Cake Sale (page 28).

As well as breaking down your audience into these three sets of people, you should think about what the different groups are like; your family may be quiet, while some sports teams like big nights out. Philanthropic clubs will be dedicated and interested in the cause, while your friends may be more interested in a new experience. Tailor your style to suit your audience.

Each Fundraising Idea (pages 32 to 101) in this book has an indication of the sort of people who enjoy and respond best to these events, but remember to always respect what people say and that some people may surprise you, so don't be afraid to experiment!

Know the Rules

Some of these are definite musts, others are good practice. We've split it into Dos and Don'ts to make it easy to read and get on with raising!

Don't

Put any money which belongs to the charity into your own bank account. This can lead to confusion and problems further down the line.

Say you're working "on behalf of" a charity unless you have a formal contract with them which agrees that you are!

Take any photos unless the people are happy for you to do so (and parents are happy for kids) or without explaining what the photos will be used for.

Let children be unsupervised, alone with anyone who hasn't been background checked or do activities without their parents' permission. More details on Child Protection can be found on page 55.

At events open to the public, you mustn't sell alcohol, run a raffle, a lottery or an auction without a licence. Don't be put off yet, though: see page 45 for details on what this really means and the Useful Links section (page 111) for further guidance.

Run a public collection without the right licence. More on how to get these on page 60.

Put up posters and banners without asking first!

As the subtitle suggests, you should never shake your bucket! It's considered intimidating and disruptive by some people so just go with a big smile and conversation instead!

Do

Clearly state that you're raising "in aid of" your cause: this means you're not claiming to work for them directly.

Claim back legitimate expenses. This can include travel costs, venue hire and publicity materials. All well established causes will have a clear policy on this: don't be afraid to ask.

Always ensure that two people count the takings and agree on the total. Record how much was raised and keep two copies of these records.

Bank the money as soon as possible and do so directly with the cause or charity.

Have good food hygiene standards. Look up the regulations online if you're particularly focusing on food sales. Different types of food and types of events have different rules.

If you're involving the public, check venues have sufficient public liability insurance for the activities you will be running if they're out of the ordinary.

Think about the risks involved in activities, write them down and plan and write down how you'll prevent them. That's it. You just made a risk assessment. See page 102 for a full guide.

Make sure you have checked the rules on temporary event notices if you want to perform live music in a public place.

Remember that the advice in this book is given with best intentions but is only a suggestion of how things can be done. None of the advice is legally binding and you should make decisions based on your own situation and seek extra help and advice where necessary.

Set Targets

If you have a particular aim for your fundraising, then it's important to plan how to get there. This is often the case in projects where you have to raise money beforehand, such as before an international volunteering project or challenge expedition, but target setting can also push you to be more effective for smaller and on-going fundraising aims.

In order to assess your progress, you need to set targets for how much money you want to raise and when you want to do it by. You may have an idea of either or both of these already. Perhaps you need £400 by June to donate to a project you're working with in the summer. If you don't already know either, think about how much fundraising experience you have, and you should also break down the time you have and make smaller targets, taking account of when you will have more or less opportunity to fundraise. Use this sample target planner and step-by-step guide to help you:

1. Write down your Final Date and Target Amount.
   £400 by 1st June

2. Calculate how much time you have between now and the final date.
   It's 5th January now, that's 5 months until June.

3. Work out roughly what 80% of this time is.
   80% of 5 months is 4 months, that's the start of May.

4. Set this 80% date as your Target Date, leaving you spare time if you've not reached your Target Amount.

5. Divide the Target Amount across the time you have: this can be done monthly or weekly depending on how much time you have.
   £400 in 4 months is £100 per month.

6. Think about when you'll have more or less opportunity to fundraise and shift your smaller targets to reflect this. Make sure the total still adds up to your Target Amount and DON'T leave it all to the last minute! Seeing lots of friends and family at Easter in March but have exams in January.

Example Target Planner:

Target Amount:	£400		
Final Date:	1st June		
Time until Final Date:	5 months	x 80% =	4 months
Target Date:	1st May		

Month	Month Target	Shifted to suit you	Total:
January	100	60	
February	100	120	
March	100	120	
April	100	100	
			400

Check page 105 in the Resources section at the back of the book for a DIY Target Planner! Now you have targets in place, you can decide what to do to get there.

Decide what to do

So you know that your friends love football and your Nan will help you by baking a cake. You know you have 4 months to do it and you want enough money for a new hospital... or a new sofa for the waiting room, at least.

Next you're going to be hit by our wonderful ideas pages and you need to keep your head as you're bombarded by inspiration and advice. So here's a little quiz to guide you through:

1. **How much fundraising have you done before?**

A. Yeah, loads, I practically ran Comic Relief last year.
B. A few car-boot sales, a tuck shop and a school fair/ I did a 5K once for sponsorship.
C. What-raising?

2. **How much time have you got on your hands?**

A. I'm really free. I have a year out to fill and I've been fundraising for this charity for years but want to get more involved.
B. I can give at least every other weekend for 3 months.
C. Well I have 5 A levels, a job and I swim for England. I'm sure that leaves about an hour a week!

3. **What are your audience like?**

A. They're always looking for the next wild idea.
B. They're really supportive and want to get stuck in. I also have a lot of links to other groups.
C. Well, I have one friend who sort of encouraged me. And I know my postman pretty well...

Mostly A

Take your pick! You obviously know what you're doing and as you need to raise a lot of money fast, if you're prepared to take a risk you can try the Go Big or Go Home pages. With friends like yours, a bungee jump (page 86) sounds like it could be a winner! Just remember, these can lose you money if they go wrong. If you're not prepared to risk it, a number of solid and well-timed events from our Step It Up pages could do the trick.

Mostly B

Step It Up! It sounds like you're ready to get stuck in. You have the time you need and the support behind you, so try running a couple of Keep It Simple ideas to get your confidence up and, as word spreads, head to the Step It Up pages to make the most of your experience! Remember to keep communicating with your friends and family to see how involved they want to be and say thank you often!

Mostly C

Keep It Simple. You need to get to grips with what fundraising involves (this book is a good start!) and build up a group of people who will support you while you do it: not necessarily with money or a lot of time, just caring how it's going is often as important. If you don't have a lot of time on your hands, you can organise these quickly between other commitments.

In reality, you might be a bit of a mix of these, so our best advice is to do a number of events, start small and grow as fast as you feel comfortable. The Challenge Event idea (page 82) sets out a good plan for how to structure a number of events in a timeframe while targeting different audiences.

Welcome to the Ideas Pages

We've tried to make these pages as easy and inspirational to read as we could. To make it really simple for you to find the right ideas for you, here's how our pages work:

The ideas are divided between three levels

Keep It Simple (page 30 to 55)
    Step It Up (page 56 to 77)
        Go Big or Go Home (page 78 to 101)

You can see from looking at the side of the book which is which as the red border gets higher.

Raise your skills

At the beginning of each level of ideas, we have additional skills ideas to keep you on top of your game as you progress up to tougher challenges. These can be useful at any stage, so don't be afraid to jump around and skill-up for the simpler initiatives too!

Raising Potential

£ = Small but low risk

££ = Potential to raise more if it works well

£££ = You could be raking it in! These often require a bigger investment to get off the ground, so can make a loss if something goes wrong. Plan carefully!

Time Scale

Each page gives you an idea of how long the preparation and execution of an event or initiative will take. With this, you can plan how to fit events into your time scale!

Aimed At

Check out our Know your Audience pages (page 20) for advice on this one. Try to vary who you target and run a range of events to keep it fresh.

Look out for the fairy lights which signify the **seasonal events**. These work best at certain times of year. Probably shouldn't plan that Santa's Grotto for July!

In 5 Steps

This gives you a basic check list of what needs to be done, in what order. It's not exhaustive, but puts you on the right track.

"Been there, done that"

Our quotes from other young fundraisers will give you their tips and tricks, their epic fails for you to avoid and their "I raised how much?!!" moments, to give you courage and fortitude!

Cost

Within the Go Big Or Go Home ideas, we also specify how much the event will cost in advance so you have an idea of what budget needs to be available to you before you start. These are calculated from real events, but all costs can vary, just as the format of events can change. Try to avoid paying costs for smaller events in advance and instead ask for the resources (such as a venue) to be donated as a gift in kind.

Committee

The Go Big Or Go Home ideas also look at the number of people you'll need to pull off each event. They've been worked out so you'll all have plenty to do without being over-burdened.

Keep it Simple Skills

Our skills pages don't only help you to be ahead of the game when it comes to fundraising, they also highlight really professional and transferable skills which can help you get to university and into a first job and will stay with you all through your life!

Say Thank You Properly

Whether you've run a bake sale or a barbecue, there will be someone who has helped you out, given you permission or just come along and enjoyed the event. Saying "Thank you" properly means acknowledging all of their involvement in making a successful event. Saying thank you also reminds people of your cause and will make them more likely to think favourably of it and potentially donate again in the future.

Get the word out

Send a hand-written thank you note to everyone who has given up time to really get involved, and get in touch with a local paper to include an article about the event which includes a big thank you to everyone who helped and came.

Give it some context

One of the most powerful ways of making supporters (and yourself) feel valuable is to equate their donation to a tangible result. This could be "your donation funded 3 new books for the local library", "the £400 we collected means an extra play session for disabled children" or "every £10 we received pays for 10 life-saving mosquito nets". If people can picture a tangible result, they'll feel much more closely involved and will trust the cause more.

Know your Competition (and make them your friends!)

You should find out what other fundraising is happening in your area, be it your uni, school, college or community. People will get 'fatigued' - or just annoyed - if they're asked too often for money, and will stop wanting to give.

Instead of going head-to-head with other fundraisers and running events or campaigns in competition, you should get in touch and find ways to work together! It could be that they're organising a Christmas fair, so ask to run a cake stall at it, or there's an existing charity club night at your uni, organise a drinks event earlier the same evening and you can get more people going to both and increase every-one's fundraising totals!

Risk Assessments

These may seem like the two most tedious words in existence, but it's really easy to write a risk assessment and is a way of organising yourself in advance in case anything does go wrong.

Sit down and write out the common risks of the event you're running, what controls you'll use to prevent them and any important contacts. So long as the risk is tolerable with the controls you put in place, then you're fine to run your event. Imagine you're running a barbecue: things like food poisoning and burns need to be planned for. Meteor strikes and riots are not risks you need to worry about!

Have a look at page 102 in the Reference section for an example risk assessment. These can sometimes be required to fulfil insurance criteria for the venue you're using, so get into the habit of writing one up and ask venues what they expect.

Keep It Simple

Cake Sale

Raising Potential	£	Time 24 hours
Aimed at	Everyone	

Of course we had to start with this one! It's the classic in fundraising and everyone loves cakes! This idea can be expanded by offering people the opportunity to decorate their own cakes or selling cakes alongside another event to guarantee a hungry crowd!

In 5 Steps

1. Find a good spot and ask permission
2. Put up some posters, tell people online, stand on a chair and shout about it.
3. Bake lots of cakes
4. Decide on pricing and make sure you have loads of small change for selling.
5. Sell the cakes!

Katie raised over £1000 for Helen and Douglas House, a children's respite hospice through cake sales.

"Don't underestimate the power of cake sales! They're a really safe way of making a good profit. My secret weapon is Smarties! Any cake will sell better if there are Smarties on top!"

Keep It Simple

Online Donations Page

Raising Potential	££	Time	1 hour per week

Aimed at	Family & Friends

These sites allow you to create a personal page which documents your progress towards a target, allows people to donate to you online as well as giving GiftAid and some even send donors an automatic thank you message. Many of these sites take a small cut of the money somehow, whether from each donation, from the final total or as an initial sign-up fee. The sites with the least cost attached are given below. Often causes have a preferred site as they've negotiated a good deal with them.

5 of the top sites are:

 www.btplc.com/mydonate

 www.bmycharity.com

 www.charitychoice.co.uk

 www.virginmoneygiving.com

 www.everyclick.com

This list comes from Moneysavingexpert.com

Fundraising Games

Raising Potential	££	Time	3 hours each

Aimed at	Everyone

If you're able to piggyback on another event, or even just looking to make the most of a crowded evening in the Students' Union, there are loads of easy games you can set up to fundraise. The great thing about these is they cost next to nothing to set up and they can be run over and over again! Here are a few to get you started, but be creative and see if you can think up any of your own!

Balance a coin on an orange

What you need: an orange, a big bowl, jug or bucket of water, some coins to set up with, plenty of willing participants.

How it works: Fill the bowl/jug/bucket with water, put the orange to float in it. Now check that if you put a coin on the orange it won't stay on for more than 20 seconds (oranges will almost always roll but some are annoyingly stable, so useless for this game!).

Now you tell people they have to put a coin on the orange and get it to stay there for 20 seconds. If they manage it, they get 5 times the value of their coin back. If not, you keep the coin.

Roll a pound at a bottle of wine

What you need: a bottle of wine (or anything else people will want to win!), a space about 5m by 2m, a hard floor, plenty of willing participants.

How it works: This one is relatively simple: you set up a line on the floor with a bottle about 5 metres away (somewhere people won't be walking and on a hard, even floor). Then as if it's a bowling alley, people have to roll pound coins towards the bottle. If they hit the bottle with their coin, they can take it home!

Pin the tail on the donkey

You probably know it as a kid's game, but what's to say you can't use it to fundraise with big kids, too? Be creative here, if you have a popular mascot you could sack off the donkey and use them instead. I once ran a great evening of pin the horn on the unicorn.

What you need: A big picture of a donkey / your chosen creature without their tail / your chosen body part, a pin-board or large cardboard backing to mount it on, a tail with a pin in it, a blindfold, a prize for the winner, plenty of willing participants.

How it works: People pay a set amount to have a go (say 50p or £1), you blindfold them, spin them around a couple of times and then point them at the board with the tail in their hands. They have a go at pinning it in the right place, you make a mark where they got it and at the end of the evening, whoever got it closest wins a prize.

Guess how many sweets in a jar

Easy peasy: you fill a big jar with sweets (remember to count them as they go in) and then people pay a small amount to guess how many sweets are in the jar. Write down all the guesses and whoever gets closest gets to keep the jar of sweets!

Keep It Simple

Get Social Media Savvy

Raising Potential	£	Time	2 hours per week

Aimed at	Family & Friends, Organisations & Groups

We all know Facebook, you probably spend too much time on there already and use it to keep up with friends. So it's a perfect tool to let them know what you're up to with your fundraising! You can also make use of the networks and resources you can find through Twitter and blogs too.

In 5 steps

1. To begin with, you can message friends on Facebook with the link to your online donations page and post it out as your status along with photos demonstrating your cause. For events, create a catchy Facebook event for each event you run and share it on any relevant groups or pages on Facebook to get the message out and get lots of people along.

2. Twitter is a really great tool to link to other interesting groups or individuals. You can set up keyword searches and explore, reply to and re-tweet tweets from others interested in the same subjects as you. It can also work to promote your events by tweeting at local media, groups or interested individuals who might share it. Remember: the more you re-tweet others, the more they will re-tweet you!

3. Think about putting together a blog: using sites like Word-Press or Blogger means they're easy to set up but you can still be creative in the design. Browse some others to get an idea of how to design your own. This is a space where you can write longer posts about your motivations, experiences and thoughts as you go. This is a great place to give more detail about your cause and why it's important to you. Get people to visit it by putting updates on Facebook and Twitter whenever you have a new post.

Keep It Simple

4   The key with all social media is to be interactive, repost/retweet things by others, reply to interesting threads and share your updates through pages and groups too. Photos and videos get a lot more views and can add loads to the 140 characters allowed by Twitter!

5   Link all the sites up! If you find something great on Twitter, talk about it in a blog and share your latest blog posts over Facebook!

Jess ran the social media for her university RAG group:

"We found Facebook was the second best way after face-to-face for getting people interested in something. A couple of weeks before a big event, the whole committee and all of our reps and friends would invite everyone we knew from the uni to an event online, we would post it as our status, on the walls of anyone who might want to come and any pages with students in who could be interested. We'd also make a promo video and post it all over Facebook too. We know we annoyed some people, but almost everyone had heard of our events!"

Keep It Simple

Top tip
If you're running a series of events, make your own brand around them with similar description styles and event pictures.

Clothes Swap

Raising Potential **££**	Time 1 day

Aimed at	Family & Friends, Organisations & Groups

In 5 Steps

1. Find a venue and decide whether you will charge for entry or per item which people take away from the event. Around £5 for entry or £2 per item (maybe more if they're especially nice) is about right.

2. Advertise to friends and family and tell them to bring anyone else who may be interested

3. On the day, make sure you have plenty of rails and hangers to display all of the items and think about selling extra things on the side like tea and cake.

4. Welcome everyone in, take their items to display them and explain the setup. Often people say you can take as many pieces as you brought or pay extra if you want to go home with more.

5. Following the event, some people may want to take home items which have not been swapped, others may donate them. These can be donated to charity if in good condition, or sold on sites like eBay if they are more valuable.

Sarah raised £45 with a simple clothes swap in her living room. The money went to Hindu Vidyapeeth, an education charity based in Nepal.

"The clothes swap was fun! I charged £2 entry and about 12 friends came. I also sold hand-made earrings and glasses of wine. We all had a good gossip, tried on loads of things and left with a new outfit each!"

Top tip If you have a free venue, the profitability of this event is much higher!

Philanthropic Group Sponsorship

Raising Potential £	Time 1 day

Aimed at	Organisations & Groups

In 5 Steps

1 See page 106 for a sample letter which you can use to draft your own.

2 Look up any groups in your local area (both your home town and university town if appropriate!): groups such as the Rotary Club, Soroptimists, Lion's Clubs, religious groups and any groups specific to your area.

3 Find a name, email address and phone number and see if you can find any instructions about applying for grants on their websites.

4 It's often worth calling a member of the board if a number is available, to ask whether your request would be considered and if they've funded similar things in the past.

5 Write a polite letter to the group. Be careful to outline the benefit your project will have to the local area, as that is often a concern to these groups. Often these groups are quite traditional, so sending it by post can be the best route. Others prefer them by email these days!

Duncan manages the Aspatria Charity Shop which donates all profits to local community projects.

"It's the community who runs the shop and we encourage groups in the community who need to fundraise to ask us. We try to avoid too many restrictions, but the committee decide quarterly who we should fund"

Keep It Simple

Poker Night

Raising Potential **££**	Time 1 day

Aimed at   **Friends & Family,** Groups & Organisations

If you've got a poker face and know enough about cards, this may seem like a lucrative way to roll in some cash. However, it's important to be aware of the legalities of running any sort of gambling.

To keep it simple, you cannot run an event where people are gambling for money without a strict licence. This doesn't mean you have to put away the chips, though, just be clever about how you frame the event.

In 5 Steps

1. People pay an entry fee to the event

2. Upon entry everyone gets a bag of chips

3. There are games available for people to play with their chips.

4. People can hand back their chips and you keep a note of who handed back the most.

5. Whoever has handed back the most chips (or the top three) wins a prize at the end of the event!

Try to get in-kind donations as your prizes: a bottle of fizz donated by your local shop or a free meal in a local restaurant. See page 18 for more details on how to get this.

If you find the poker lifestyle is one for you, take a look at page 72 for our Step It Up idea to Rent a Casino.

Keep It Simple

Collection Tins

Raising Potential £	Time 6 easy months
Aimed at Everyone	

You've probably seen collection tins for charities in local shops, pubs and cafés for people's spare change. This is a really effort-free way to make some cash, especially if it's a local cause which people recognise and you can have tins in a few places.

Imagine you have 5 tins in shops around town. Each month they get £10 each in them. It's not a lot, but together that's £50 a month and over 6 months, you've got £300 just for asking the shop owner and saying thank you at the end!

However there are a few legalities around this. The tin must be secure and tamper-proof. This usually means having a signed and dated sticker over the opening to the tin. If the charity has someone responsible for fundraising, they will be able to give you a sealed tin which is returned to them (still sealed) when full. There are no licences needed to leave them anywhere, you just need to have permission from the business owner.

Remember this is the perfect opportunity to say thank you properly and build positive feeling. Send a hand-written letter to whichever shops or businesses have let you have your collection tin there and drop it off personally. A box of chocs usually goes down well, too!

Keep It Simple

Do Something Silly for Sponsorship

Raising Potential ££	Time 1 week

| Aimed at   Everyone | |

This one relies on timing. If your school, college or university has a Charity Week or RAG Week, that's perfect. Otherwise, in the run-up to a holiday is good, so before Easter or Christmas, as most people get distracted by exams before the summer.

Try to choose something eye-catching. Often doing something strange over a few days means there's time for people to hear about it, find you to see if it's for real, then donate. Use a sponsorship form: they can promise one donation for completion or an amount per day you keep going. See Resources on page 110 for an example form.

Publicise before, during and after: put a sign on yourself which explains what you're doing and who you're raising for. Carry a collecting can during the challenge, too, for any spur-of-the-moment donations. Remember to be thick-skinned: people will give you strange looks but it will be worth it!

Dan shaved his long hair off for charity:

"I shaved my head for my university RAG society. I hit up all of my friends, peers and family for donations, going all out, conscious that I wouldn't be able to ask people for sponsorship again for a while after this and come away with any friends left. I also gave my hair to a charity that makes wigs for children with cancer, which meant it had to be in small braids. I charged people £1 for the privilege of snipping one off, to make some extra money, and got match funding from my college. All in all, I raised £1,500"

Keep It Simple

Easter Egg Hunt

Raising Potential £	Time 2 days

Aimed at	Friends & Family, Organisations & Groups

In 5 Steps

1 Find a venue- a big field is great!

2 Find an audience (kids love this: if you can get a school or after school club involved where everyone is happy to pay £1, you're on to a winner!)

3 Buy loads of Easter goodies!

4 You can either hide them and let people loose to gather them up or use clues to direct competing teams or individuals between the hidden treats.

5 Make a day out of it and run bunny-hopping competitions, egg and spoon races and other fun things alongside!

Watch out! While this is great fun, leaving chocolate in a field can lead to problems...

"I was running an Easter egg hunt last year and was really worried about animals in the park eating the chocolate so I hid them in jam jars - with enough chocolate for each team to take one from each jar. Two things went wrong. We didn't put lids on the jars and it rained heavily before... we had very soggy chocolate! And then the teams all just took the whole jars, so loads of them were missing for other teams! We started it again but learnt the value of clear instructions!"

Keep It Simple

Supermarket Bag Pack

Raising Potential **££**	Time 1 day

Aimed at   Everyone

Its worth approaching local supermarkets to see if they are happy for you to do this: Saturday mornings always work best for profitability, and the bigger the group of packers, the better. Face to face is best: ask to speak to the store manager and (while many say no) those who say yes are usually very helpful. Be warned, though, the earliest available date is usually a couple of months away.

5 Top Tips

1 Always ask people if they're happy for you to help and spend the time explaining your cause.

2 Let the donation be optional and discretionary. A bucket on the checkout which you can point out politely means people can choose whether they want to donate and how much without pressure.

3 Don't do this while you're hungry or you'll be tempted to spend more than you earn on supermarket snacks!

4 Wear a T-shirt which explains your cause and take some leaflets or tell people the website to visit if they're interested in learning more.

5 Be conversational: people like nice people and you'll get bored very quickly if you don't make some (very short-term) friends!

Keep It Simple

Raffle

Raising Potential ££	Time 2 days

Aimed at	Organisations & Groups

Raffles are best when 'piggybacking' on events where there will already be lots of people, so this would be a great add-on to a Charity Ball (page 90) or Car Boot Sale (page 60) where they're happy for you to fundraise.

In 5 Steps

1 Think about prizes. Good prizes mean more people will play and will pay more for a ticket. Use the sponsorship letter in the Resources section (page 106) to approach local shops and get things for free in return for promoting them at the event.

2 Buy raffle ticket books and decide whether you'll need to take names, phone numbers, addresses, etc. depending on when you're doing the draw and giving out or delivering prizes.

3 Set out all of the prizes for people to see and anything promised (like a spa treatment) can be written or presented as a voucher. Decide on pricing to buy a ticket.

4 Encourage lots of people to buy tickets!

5 Draw the prizes. If people are there, they can come up and choose their prize as they're drawn, otherwise they can be assigned in the order people are drawn.

Keep it Legal

The time frame you hold your raffle over is really important, if you're selling tickets and drawing the winners within 24 hours, you're fine, but if it's over a longer period, you must apply for a Small Lottery Licence from your local council.

Keep It Simple

Valentine's Day Roses

Raising Potential ££	Time 1 month

Aimed at	Friends & Family, Organisations & Groups

Raise money. Spread love. Win.

In 5 Steps

1 Plan ahead of time and really think through how many people will want to join in. This works really well at school, before everyone is matched up or thinks they're too cool.

2 Approach a number of florists early (right after Christmas is about right!). Get quotes for the number of roses you want and try to barter as you're buying in bulk: remember to factor in the price you'll be selling them for so your profit is worth the effort you're putting in.

3 Set up a stall to take orders and collect money, and do it online as well if you want to increase reach, then label up the roses and distribute them. A cupid costume always comes in handy about now!

4 You can deliver them anonymously, with messages, riddles or contact details for a first date!

5 Sit back and watch the love blossom! If this goes well and you want to step up your romantic raising, see page 64 for Blind Date.

Top tip

This idea can work just as well at Christmas with candy canes: they're cheaper and last longer than roses too!

Keep It Simple

Make a Recipe Book

Raising Potential £	Time 2 weeks

Aimed at Everyone	

This is a great idea for anyone who loves to bake or cook and it could be sold at bake sales alongside dishes listed in the book! If someone comes to love a recipe in your book, they're bound to tell people about the book it was in and raise the profile of your cause at the same time. Don't expect to be the next Mary Berry, but it could be a steady earner for the right cause.

In 5 Steps

1. This will work best when you know some really good, diverse or unique cooks and an audience who would be interested in buying it, or an event to sell them: a food fair would be perfect!

2. Ask them if they'll share their recipes and write them all down.

3. See if you can get someone to make the recipes and photograph them well or ask someone to illustrate the book.

4. Compile it all! Make sure to include a page about the cause and either print them yourself (expect £2-3 per book) or get them done professionally and charge a bit more.

5. Sell them! To supporters, friends and family, at local events and online through social media are the best routes!

Keep It Simple

Barbecue

Raising Potential ££	Time 2 days
Aimed at Everyone	

Sunny days and hot dogs are made for each other.

In 5 Steps

1 Find a venue (look below for advice on piggybacking!)

2 Write a risk assessment (more details below)

3 Think logistics: How will you get the barbecue there? How will you keep the meat cold? What will you serve for vegetarians? (Remember to use a separate cooking grill and utensils for the vegetarian items.) Do you want to do drinks, too?

4 Plan roles. Avoid fights over who uses the tongs. Make sure you have enough people and defined roles.

5 Get lots of small change in advance, make some posters of prices and start barbecueing!

This is so easy to do when you're piggybacking on someone else's event (see page 19 for a definition of piggybacking). So if you know of sports events or summer fetes coming up, approach them and explain your cause and ask to run a barbecue. It's good to get in well in advance so they've not planned one themselves.

This is a really important event to do a risk assessment for. See page 31 for an explanation of what this involves and page 102 for a sample risk assessment. Key things to think about are how you will keep everything cool before cooking, make sure it's all cooked properly and not let anyone burn themselves. For more advice on food safety, you can also visit www.food.gov.uk.

Keep It Simple

Restaurant Night

Raising Potential £	Time 1 week

Aimed at Everyone

We've been talking a fair bit about gifts in kind and raising goodwill as well as money. This basically means someone notices your cause and thinks nice things about it on one day, so are more likely to donate on another day. A restaurant night is a perfect way to both optimise on the goodwill already out there and build some more!

You're basically asking a restaurant to spend one night running as usual but telling people about the cause and donating some profits to it!

So what should you do?

1 Approach locally owned restaurants as they can make their own decisions more easily than large chains. It's even better if whoever runs the restaurant is already a supporter of the cause.

2 Agree what you'll do for them. It could be you promise a party of 10 people on a quiet night or you advertise the restaurant within your club, group, company, school, university, etc.

3 Agree what they'll do for you. 10% of their profits from one night or all proceeds from a certain dish or drink are really good ideas.

This is great practice at negotiation and you can get some great results by being friendly, confident and professional. If you do this well, it can really work well for job and uni applications. See the reference section for how to do this. See page 61 for Dinner Party to step this idea up!

Keep It Simple

Teach Someone

Raising Potential £	Time 1 hour a week

Aimed at Everyone

In 5 Steps

1 Decide what it is you're good at. It could be academic tutoring, swimming, knitting, bike maintenance, cooking...

2 Decide who you want to teach. Thinking you'll be tutoring GCSE Spanish and getting 4 year olds who still don't know enough English words isn't easy.

3 Advertise yourself! There are loads of tutoring agencies online who take a percentage of what you earn or charge a fee to sign up, or you can put an advert out on Gumtree, in a local newspaper, in local shops, community centres or schools.

4 If you want to become more serious, try hosting a weekly class. Remember to factor in the cost of renting a space. Word might spread and you'll be making a lot of money!

5 Remember that if the money does not all go directly to the charity, it may need to be declared as income to be taxed. Check the legalities if you start getting serious!

Rebekah raised over £500 for Jacari, an education charity.

"I was already tutoring a child through Jacari for free and I decided to tutor privately, too, and donate the extra money to Jacari! It's a fun job to inspire a child to learn and it was easy to find tutoring work."

Step Up this idea - check out page 59 for how you can Use your Skills even more effectively!

Car Wash

Raising Potential ££	Time 1 day
Aimed at Everyone	

A car wash is really entrepreneurial and can take a variety of forms. The first is to set up shop somewhere with lots of passing cars: a supermarket carpark would be perfect if you can get permission. The second is to be on the move: you can go door to door to offer your services locally. Either way, make sure you're well prepared and ready for a hard day's work!

Top car washing tips from Craig, a proud car owner (also the author's Dad)

1 Start from the top down so the dirty water isn't dripping over the clean bits

2 Remember to do the wheels and tyres. They're usually the muddiest, so using a washing-up brush is a good move, then polish them with a softer cloth.

3 Once you've done the windows, dry them off properly with a clean tea-towel to stop any smears.

4 If you want to offer the full service, get a cheap hoover and clean inside the car, too.

Think about and budget for the things you'll need to buy: buckets, cloths, brushes and any detergents. From this, work out how many cars you'll have to clean to pay this back and be in profit and how long this will take you. This will help to determine how profitable this initiative will be for you!

Keep It Simple

Pumpkin Carving Competition

Raising Potential £	Time 1 day

Aimed at	Friends & Family, Groups & Organisations

In 5 steps

1. Find a space and advertise the event. You may also want a guest judge, so ask them early and think about getting a prize as a gift-in-kind from a local shop or restaurant who can sponsor the event.

2. Buy pumpkins! Remember to also provide candles for inside them, bins and black sacks for all the carved-out seeds and flesh and knives to do the carving. On that note, this isn't a wise event for young children.

3. Set your prices and time scale for the carving.

4. Welcome everyone, hand out the pumpkins and watch the designs develop.

5. Display all the pumpkins with candles inside for the judging: beware of fire regulations for this bit!

Francesca ran a pumpkin carving event in Oxford but bought too many pumpkins, and when only a handful of people turned up, she hadn't covered the cost. The event was quiet but fun, but the next morning she contacted loads of other societies in the university and found some who were running Halloween parties that night and agreed to buy them off her, meaning she did make a profit in the end! Her advice for any event is:

"Find out how many people are coming before you splash out on buying everything - and be prepared to think on your feet!"

Keep It Simple

Christmas Card Requests

| Raising Potential £ | Time 2 hours |

| Aimed at | Friends & Family |

In 5 Steps

1. Decide who you think is appropriate to send a request to. Often families have strong feelings about how relatives and old friends should be contacted, so be respectful.

2. Write a letter which explains what you're doing and why you're passionate about it. This is the place to show your personal attachment to a cause.

3. You can choose to include your online giving website or a way to donate or be more subtle and simply say "donations all go to...", people can then post a donation back or get in touch for more details if they want to donate.

4. Send the letters inside your Christmas cards.

5. If Christmas is the time for giving, it's also the time for saying Thank You. Send lots of cards to do this, too!

Ollie raised over £200 for his World Challenge this way:

"My Mum knew we had a lot of family who would really love to hear about World Challenge, so I put a letter in all of our Christmas cards explaining what I was doing and it mentioned at the bottom I was fundraising and donations would go to the charity project. It turns out some of our relatives had come into money and other friends and relatives were feeling generous. I got over £200 in cheques through the post!"

Keep It Simple

Christmas Present Wrapping Service

Raising Potential £	Time 1 day

Aimed at   Everyone

Think about where people with presents will be: at a Christmas market, on a high street, in a shopping centre. You'll need to get permission from a local council to set up a wrapping service in any public space, and from the owners or managers of any private space.

In 5 Steps

1 Get permission to set up a wrapping station somewhere busy.

2 Buy everything you need. Don't scrimp on quality: it's worth a pound more for good paper and some ribbons or you'll get a reputation for being cheap. Don't forget the tape and scissors!

3 Set your pricing and decide how long you'll need before people return for their packages. Think about charging per present, with large or awkward packages costing a bit more.

4 Make sure you have plenty of hands available: if you get a big pile to wrap, you'll need to do so quickly!

5 Don't mix up the gifts! Come up with a system so once they're wrapped, that power tool for Dad and Auntie Barbara's new vase end up with the right people!

Santa's Grotto

Raising Potential ££	Time 2 days
Aimed at Everyone	

This event is a winner every Christmas time, whether it's for little brothers and sisters at school or for the big kids at the Students' Union at University! Make sure to give people something for their money: an age-appropriate gift and a photo emailed or put on Facebook afterwards are great ideas! With young children, Santa needs to look authentic and take his role seriously, but for big kids at uni, he can have some more fun!

Any space can become a Grotto, if you buy some red material (old curtains from a charity shop would be great!) to drape over the walls, or even decorate a corner of a bigger room. Fake snow, a Christmas tree and some reindeer props go a long way, too. And don't forget to invite Santa with his bushy beard and his outfit!

Child protection

While this is a great event, to keep kids safe and you clear of any problems, you must never leave a child alone or with people who have not had a DBS check (this used to be called a CRB). The easiest thing to do is to ask their parents to be with them at all times. Failing that, Santa or someone else in the grotto should be DBS checked (this can be done by most charities but takes a few weeks to process) or the Grotto should be set up so it's open onto another space where other people will always be and you're therefore never alone with a child. See page 111 in the Reference section to full links to child protection resources.

Keep It Simple

Step it Up Skills

Bigger initiatives need a more sophisticated input. This section explains practical ways to be more efficient and productive as you develop your leadership. It will not only give you skills for fundraising; these skills are really important in life more generally and in the workplace, too, and can make you stand out to employers.

Marketing

Elevator Pitch

Need to get your point across better? Explain your initiative in 1 minute, as if you only have someone's attention for the length of an elevator ride. Now do it again, making sure you are telling them the event, the cause and one reason they should be involved. Now do it with pauses for breath, too: you'll soon cut out all of the unnecessary waffle!

Get in the Press

Help get word out about the cause as well as individual events by getting in the local press. Local newspapers and radio stations are always looking for stories, and university newspapers are a great way of engaging the student audience. Think about who your target audience is to get the right media. Next, write a few paragraphs explaining who you are, what you're doing and why. They might want to run a story before an event or after: if it's after, send some photos, too. Either way, you're getting word out!

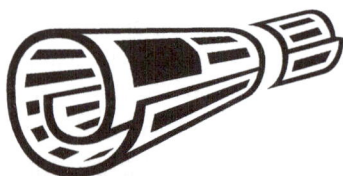

Teamwork

You may already be in a team for your fundraising or you may have decided to form one to help you out (if so, check out page 78). Either way, here is one fun and one practical strategy to get the most from your team.

Spaghetti-Marshmallow Tower

This will teach you who takes what role in the team and how well you work together under pressure. Within the team, you have 10 pieces of dry spaghetti, one marshmallow and 50cm tape. You have 5 minutes to build the tallest tower you can. Some people will immediately take the lead, others will be quieter and more strategic, others will be great at the practical assembly, and some will thrive on being given good instruction. These roles are not set in stone but in 5 minutes you can get a really good idea of team dynamics!

Productive Team Meetings

Without direction, it's very easy to have a meeting which gets nothing done. Everyone leaves more confused than before and you're going backwards! These 5 tips should help:

1   Set a plan of what you'll talk about before and make sure everyone has seen it.

2   If you've not worked together before, introduce yourselves properly and explain why you each want to be there.

3   Someone should take notes of all decisions made, action points and who will carry these out.

4   Sometimes quick decisions are good decisions. Think stuff through, but keep the pace moving.

5   Biscuits always help!

Budgeting

Now you're planning bigger events, you will be investing more time and money in advance, so it's important to know what you expect to make in different scenarios.

The best tool to do this is Microsoft Excel (and knowledge of Excel will set you apart to employers, too) but for a simple budget, you can achieve the same result with a pen and paper. This simple budget will give you a starting point, and see page 104 for a blank version for you to work through.

Budget for Dinner Party

Expenditure		Income	
Dinner Ingredients	£120	Ticket Sales	£300
Wine	£40	Raffle	£10
Decorations	£10		
Totals	**£170**		**£310**
Profit = Income - Expenditure			£140

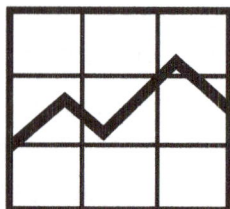

Use your Skills

Raising Potential ££	Time 1 day to 1 year

Aimed at Everyone

Do you have a skill which someone else would pay for? This isn't just about fundraising, but becoming a self-made entrepreneur for a good cause!

4 top marketable skills

Photography If you can get the kit and have the right skills, start by offering to photograph events for an optional donation, and as you build a portfolio, start charging more professional prices.

Web Design Know your HTML from your CSS? There are hundreds of small groups, businesses and even university societies who need websites built or updated but often don't have the skills. Advertise widely and make some examples to show off!

Gardening Mow those lawns, trim those trees! Loads of people need help with their gardens, and if you're good you'll be asked back.

Dance/ Boxing/ Yoga Why not speak to a local gym about delivering a class? They should know the laws on health and safety and they can help to advertise the class and the cause!

You can aid a lot of causes by giving your time directly as well as by fundraising. Maybe the charity needs a new website or an old people's home wants the garden doing up. This could actually save them loads of money and so be more time-effective than fundraising. Remember to share your skills with whoever you're trying to help: ask how you can be most useful!

Car Boot Sale

Raising Potential ££	Time 2 weeks
Aimed at Everyone	

This is a great event if you can partner up with a school for use of the car park or field. Make sure to advertise well in advance: a perfect opportunity to get your cause in the local press. And the great thing about this event is everyone involved leaves with a profit or a bargain, so you can build loads of positive relationships with people.

The standard format goes...
People pay around £5 to £10 to have a space for their car if they're selling. They pay as they come in and can set up for about an hour before everyone else arrives. Then more people come in (for free) to buy stuff and everyone goes home happy. Advertising is key, as you need both plenty of sellers and plenty of buyers.

For added profit try...
Head back to the Keep it Simple ideas and throw some of these in as stalls. The Barbecue (page 48), Cake Sale (page 32) and Raffle (page 45) could all be winners at a car boot sale. And the hard part of finding a venue is already covered. Make sure you have some friends to help out, though!

Top Tip
This is a great time to build people's affinity to your cause. Give out flyers with more information of who you are raising for and why and you can even get donations of items from stall holders for future events or ask for donations in kind of time spent volunteering. Face to face is the best way to spread the word about your cause, so make the most of this!

Dinner Party

Raising Potential £	Time 12 hours

Aimed at   Friends & Family

So you're a hostess with the mostest? Make an event out of it, raise money and awareness, and your friends will be paying less than for a meal in a restaurant.

Here's how it worked for Francesca

"This was my parents' idea when I was raising money for a Ugandan charity I was going to volunteer with in the summer. We invited family friends from both generations. I bought all the ingredients and each family gave £40 - so about £10 a head. I spent altogether around £25 on ingredients and my parents helped me to make everything and gave me some of their wine for us to have during the evening. Because there were 16 of us, I made a profit of £135 just for an afternoon of cooking with my parents!

It was a really great night to get support as well. I ran a quiz about Uganda and we spent ages talking about what the cause would be doing, so my friends and their parents offered to help out for other events I ran the same year."

Check back to page 58 for budgeting advice and make sure to count how long the preparation will take you before you decide whether this is the right event for you!

Sell Something the Smart Way

Raising Potential £	Time 1 day

Aimed at	Everyone

In the olden days you'd have to set up a market stall on your local high street. Now there are thousands of ways of selling things, whether it's unwanted items from around the house, a unique craft item you've created or sourcing rare finds and selling them on. From car boot sales to eBay, market stalls to auction houses, tailor your selling to the quality of item and your audience and you'll get a better price.

What to sell where

What	Online	In Person
Vintage Clothes	ASOS Marketplace	Fashion markets
Old CDs and DVDs	eBay, musicmagpie.co.uk	Car boot sales
Furniture	Gumtree, eBay	Auction houses
Bric-a-brac	eBay	Car boot sales
Vinyl disks	Specialist music stores	discogs.com, htfr.com
Home-made items	Etsy	Craft fairs, to independent shops
Books	Amazon, eBay	Second-hand book shops, car boot

If you get through all of your own stuff to sell, think about trying to source some more. Put out notices to ask for unwanted items and explain the cause that they'll be going to help. Or, to Step It Up again, you could work with your Students' Union to make a campaign across campus to collect furniture as people move out of halls or text books as people graduate. You could have drop-off points around campus and sell them on to the next generation of students at a reasonable price, with proceeds going to charity. Not only are you fundraising for your cause, you're doing your bit for the planet by recycling and helping other young people to save some money by buying second hand!

Think it through...

Selling things is a great way of making money, but just remember that causes could need more than cash. The right vinyl disk could make a wonderful gift for a retirement home. Mobile phones could help farmers in developing countries, and children's services could be in need of more books or toys. Remember to ask someone close to the cause. Sometimes the budget total isn't the only or the best way of contributing.

Blind Date

Raising Potential	££	Time 4 weeks

Aimed at	Everyone (students!)

This is perfect for Valentine's Day and for big groups like across a university or large college. There are a few ways to do it, but this one has proved a winner before:

The system is based on people filling in fun forms about themselves and their preferences in a date partner and returning them with a donation in order for you to match them with someone. You then send each dater the form belonging to the person they'll be meeting and they're free to arrange it as they like.

You can do the forms online using tools like Google docs or Survey Monkey with donations to an online giving page or in hard copy dropped off somewhere specific on campus. Just make sure you've got the donation off everyone before they're paired up.

Some example questions for the form

What year are you in?	Try to match people of about the same age range.
What halls are you at?	Try to avoid people who could know each other already (from halls or lectures)
What subject do you study?	
What is your gender?	Make sure you're matching people with the right gender for their sexual orientation!
What is your sexual orientation?	

Then add some funny questions of your own like these and have fun pairing up the responses.

If you were a drink, what would you be and why?

Describe your perfect date

Describe your worst imaginable date

What three things would you save if your house was burning down?

Which celebrity are you most like and why?

Plan your time well in advance: you'll need to fit all this in

1   Advertising Blind Date

2   Getting the forms distributed

3   Getting them back completed and with the donation (and plan how this will happen so it's easy for them but money can't get lost)

4   Matching them: the most fun but most time-consuming part.

5   Getting the matched forms back to the opposite people.

6   Letting them organise their dates.

All before Valentine's Day!

To give an extra incentive, you can ask local bars and restaurants for discounts for any couple who shows their Blind Date forms during that week. Then they have easy date locations sorted, too.

Now just sit back and wait for the wedding invitations!

Street Collection/ Raid

Raising Potential ££	Time planning + 1 day
Aimed at Everyone	

This is the classic image people have when they think of student fundraisers: keen faces and buckets on high streets. So get out there and remember: never shake your bucket!

Top Tips

1 To collect in a public place, you need to get a permit from your local council a couple of months in advance. To collect in private places (like shopping centres) you only need permission from the owners.

2 Dress up silly! The weirder you look, the more attention and more donations you'll get. Animal onesies were basically invented for this purpose!

3 Smile and say hello and don't be put off when some people ignore you, just focus on those who don't!

This is a key moment for knowing your cause. Make sure that you have a really good Elevator Pitch (see page 56) to explain yourself to busy people and that you can explain where the money will be going more thoroughly if anyone quizzes you on it.

"I once did a raid and only knew the charity worked in international conflict zones. When one passer-by asked about them, I guessed "They send experts to areas neglected by the UN to build links between opposing groups". I thought I was pretty convincing until he said "I work for the UN, where exactly is this charity working?" I had to admit I didn't know really. He didn't mind but I could have done so much damage to the cause!"

Art Show

Raising Potential ££	Time 1 month
Aimed at Everyone	

This was a winner at my school because each year students would make their GCSE and A Level final pieces for Art and Design and would get their (hopefully shining) grades but then have only one or two bits they wanted to keep. So a group at school made a website and held an art show in the school hall one weekend and loads of people came. They only sold a small volume, but each piece can be priced quite high and they got it all for free!

They charged between £5 and £50 depending on the piece, how big it was and how good it looked, and together with their website sales, they made a few hundred pounds.

Step this up

Don't just hold the show: print off a catalogue of the best bits and take it to local offices, restaurants, show homes of new build houses; anyone who might need their space brightening up with some art made by local young people which gives 100% of profits to a good cause.

To put together a catalogue, make sure you include high-quality photos and see if a local printers will make some glossy copies for you as a donation-in-kind (or see page 111 for good value ethical printing). Give it the personal touch by having descriptions of the art by the artists and remember to include information about your cause.

Corporate Sponsorship

Raising Potential **££**	Time 2 days
Aimed at	**Groups & Organisations**

Once you're getting into the realms of Corporate Sponsorship, you need to be a really professional group. A lot of what corporates - that's banks, big businesses and companies - are looking for is agreed exposure to an audience. If you're big on a university campus, you have access to thousands of potential future graduates who will be looking for jobs and these businesses want them to apply!

Common agreements for sponsorship are that the sponsorship money will pay for overheads of events, not be donated directly and that you'll have to do a certain amount of publicity for that organisation. This could mean putting their name on all of your emails, their logo on your hoodies and even hosting their people at your events.

To write a winning sponsorship letter

To make it easy for you, we've got an example letter on page 106, but read on to understand how this works.

Find the name of the right person in the company. Most places have someone who looks after their Corporate Social Responsibility and they may have a budget to share.

Next, make sure you find ways to link the work of your charity to the values or ethics of the company. To be quite honest, this can be a bit tenuous, but it's important to do in order to make whoever reads your letter feel an affinity to your cause.

Try and spell out how many people you can influence,

whether that's on a mailing list or the number of people on your campus. Stating how many people came to your biggest event is a great statistic and it's also worth outlining exactly what sort of people these are (uni students, sports teams, specific groups, school students, parents, etc.)

Specify what it is you want. While a lot of us feel that asking outright for things - especially money - is rude, if they don't know what you want, how can they give it to you? State an amount of support you're looking for and put this in terms of what events it would let you put on and how much in turn these could raise for the cause. Next, explain the ways in which you will share their name and logo at these events.

Think through the ethics of any organisations you approach. It's important that you are not receiving money from anyone who is working in a way which is at odds to your cause. If you're raising for a lung charity and it turns out your sponsor is a major investor in tobacco, it's very bad news. A lot of charities will not accept money generated through Arms or Tobacco and some avoid non-renewable energies too.

Here's what Caroline, who founded the London Climate Forum as a student, has to say about sponsorship:

"Sponsorship can be a great way to raise money to fund an event or initiative. Larger companies and organisations often have funds allocated for corporate social responsibility initiatives that you may be able to access. The key is to be organised and professional. Ask for funding well in advance of when you need it - it can take several weeks or months to process an agreement. In addition, make sure that you have a clear proposal. How much funding do you need? What will it be used for? What will the sponsor get out of it? These are all key questions to ask yourself before writing a sponsorship proposal."

Create a Calendar

Raising Potential ££	Time 1 month

Aimed at	Groups & Organisations

This can realistically go one of two ways:

1 **A calendar.** Of local landmarks, school or uni events, traditions and all-round wholesome stuff which your Mum would be proud to hang on her wall.

2 **A naked calendar.** We all know how successful the Calendar Girls were! However, this should NEVER be considered if you, your audience or (especially) anyone in the calendar is under the age of 18. There are serious laws against all of these, even though all the bits are artistically out of sight. You should also go through the proper channels of permission so you don't end up getting kicked out of whatever education establishment you're a part of.

So how to do it?

Once you have the photos (think carefully and if you're going with option 2, don't be too indecent!) its easy to get these printed into a calendar. Crucially for your eventual earnings, the more you get printed, the cheaper they are per item. However, this is only a good thing if you can actually sell them all!

There are lots of websites where you can just upload the photos and choose the template, but if you find a local printers and speak to the manager face to face, you may be able to negotiate a discount. One good way of doing this (if you're happy to) is to offer to put the logo of the printing shop on each page. If you can assure that they'll sell, you may get a number for free! Alternatively, see page 111 for good value, ethical printing companies.

Club Night

Raising Potential **££**	Time 2 weeks
Aimed at **Anyone and Everyone (over 18)**	

The perfect student event. Get organised in advance, you'll need to get a club to agree to dedicate an evening to your cause.

Often the deal is if it's usually a quiet night, you can have all of the money from the door if you make sure a minimum spend goes through the bar. Other clubs might say you can have it for a set price for the night, they'll run the bar as usual and you have to cover the door, DJ and any promotional stuff you want. Everywhere is different, but if you do a good job once you'll usually be trusted to do the same thing again and it could become a weekly event.

Think about

1   Themed nights. Think Halloween, Christmas, Valentine's Day or just cartoon characters, tight and bright, cops and robbers. Anything fancy dress is a lot more entertaining

2   Promote the night and think carefully about who you should influence to get lots of people along. A sports team who always go out that night? A Big Name On Campus who's having a birthday party and will want to go dancing after?

3   Assuming the club says it's fine, think about promotions for the evening. So a ticket is £3 if bought in advance or £5 on the door, or cheaper before 11pm.

4   If you're in charge of the DJ, make sure they can hack it! If you run one great night, people will come back for more. But if the music is poor, you might make some money but you could ruin your reputation.

Rent a Casino

Raising Potential **££**	Time 6 hours per event
Aimed at **Groups & Organisations**	

Following on from the Poker Night idea (page 40), this is a way of presenting a gambling night without any real gambling going on. Effectively, it's just a ticketed event with a set entry fee. The event then gives you free chips and games to play, and whoever hands back the most chips gets a prize at the end of the event. Simple!

So that's us covered in terms of the legalities: next it's logistics! The more professional you want to come across, the more you can charge, but the more you will have to pay out to begin with.

Here are the things you might need
Lots of chips (of the casino kind, not the with-gravy kind)
Rakes
Roulette wheel and mat (to go on any table)
Cards and dispensers
Blackjack mat (for any table)
Poker mat (for any table)
See page 111 for suggested suppliers of all this kit.

Obviously, you don't need to offer all of this to start out, you can invest in a wider range and better quality equipment as you grow in profits and popularity. That way you'll also be sure of more bookings as you make the investment and there is less risk of losing money.

So who will be running your casino? You need to recruit and train some croupiers! Some people may already be interested in casino games and know their stuff, which is great, others can be attracted by the fact you can get them into great events for free and others by the idea they're having fun for a good cause. Try to recruit a number of people at a time so you can train them in all of the games (as well as roles like front of house) at once and save yourself some time. Then it's worth deciding on a system to get the right number of croupiers at each event, whether it's a sign-up form sent around a few weeks in advance or done on a first-come-first-served basis before each event.

So now you're ready to market your casino! Think about your pricing structure: you should think through how many people you'll need and how many hours' work you'll be doing and set the price accordingly. Have a look at the suggested pricing structure below as a guide.

For kit only (consider also charging a deposit in case anything gets broken)

	Number of Hours				
Number of Games	1	2	3	4	5
1	20	40	60	80	100
2	40	80	120	160	200
3	60	120	180	240	300
4	80	160	240	320	400

For kit and croupiers (have 2 croupiers per game and 2 on front of house then double this if you're running for 4 hours or more so you can do shifts of one hour on, one hour off)

	Number of Hours				
Number of Games	1	2	3	4	5
1	50	70	90	140	160
2	90	130	170	260	300
3	130	190	250	380	440
4	170	250	330	500	580

Happy (not) gambling!

Auction of Promises

Raising Potential	**££**	Time 1 week

Aimed at	**Friends & Family, Groups & Organisations**

A great event to get people standing up and offering to do silly things for your cause! The format is like an auction you see on telly with an audience out-bidding each other and someone at the front shouting "Going, going, GONE!" However, instead of auctioning off old paintings or furniture, you're auctioning promises from people. This could be a promise to bake you a cake or to clean your room, even a cheeky kiss or to serenade you with a song. The options are endless and it's up to the crowd to think up their promises, but it's good to give people a few ideas and spark their creativity.

Rebekah ran an Auction of Promises at University:

"We sold tickets for everyone to come at £1 so it's really affordable but that way you can guarantee most of them will turn up. Then we also kept all the winning auction pledges so it was really profitable. It also helped that it was in the college bar, so people were getting a lot of drinks in and by the end they were pledging very generously! We started with things like 'I'll bake you a cake of your choice' and by the end people were offering up things like their room as a hotel for the weekend when any one else had friends to stay or to prepare every meal for someone for a week! I don't know how far all of the promises got, but we raised about £700 from putting it on, so the charity was very happy!"

This Town's Got Talent

Raising Potential	£££	Time	1 month

Aimed at	Friends & Family, Groups & Organisations

This is the classic talent show event. You can call it anything you like and obviously depending on the audience make it as well behaved or raucous as it deserves to be! It's a simple format: secure your acts (perhaps through smaller events across Halls or lots of local schools), book the venue and sell tickets! Make sure you have support in place for things like sound and lighting - will the venue have a sound system or do you need to bring your own? It's really important that you test-run this so you're happy that everyone will be able to hear, there will definitely be enough microphones and someone can be there on the day to fix any last minute issues ready for the show. Don't forget a great host or hostess for the evening and some music for before and during any intervals, as well as some snazzy sound and lighting effects as each act takes to the stage!

Think about how you can add in extra piggybacking opportunities to the event. So sell drinks and food alongside, sell memorabilia of the acts, even. This is a great time to co-ordinate with other fundraising groups. If you're busy running the event, they could provide the drinks and food.

You might like the hands in the air or the loudest scream style of voting but you can get creative and make an extra few pounds here, too. If the ticket price was set quite low, you can run the voting by having buckets for each act and whichever is most full of cash by the end of the night wins! It gets everyone digging deep in their purses as well as sparking some good old-fashioned competition, as everyone wants to see their friend win!

Hold a Christmas Market

Raising Potential ££	Time 1 month to plan

Aimed at	Friends & Family, Groups & Organisations

James and his friends ran a Christmas market to raise funds for his Sea Cadets group.

This is how they did it

"We're raising money for a new minibus and we've been doing a few different things like a bag pack and tuck shops but we decided to do this one at Christmas time. We got the hall for free because we're a local kids' group and one of the leaders knows the people who run it.

So then we all had to invite people to have stalls. It was some businesses and shops who were selling extra things at the market and some people who just make jams or stuff at home and then some charities and other groups like us as well, so the Guides came along and sold stuff for them to make money too.

The money came from charging £10 for the other people to have stalls and 50p for anyone to come in. Then we had our own tuck shop there, too, which was right at the front so it was the first thing people saw.

We had to work really hard on the day but there are 20 of us so it wasn't too bad and we could get a lot of people along because so many of us were involved. In the end we raised just over £1000! So only about £19000 to go until we can get a new minibus!"

Go Big or Go Home Skills

This is where we get serious. You'll be working in teams, even running and training them, you'll need water-tight budgets and marketing planned better than the Moon landings.

Delegation

This seems like a simple idea - asking others to help you out - but for the over-achievers of the world, it can seem like a failure if you're not doing it all yourself. And if you've got this far alongside your studies, you're probably over-achieving on some level (well done you!). The main skill in delegation comes from acknowledging the true size of any workload. This needs to be done for the full length of a project, not just the coming days and weeks.

Let's take the Bungee Jump (page 86) as an example...

You can split up the major tasks over the coming weeks as follows:

Time	Tasks
Now to Week 2	Booking event, sponsorship, budgeting, marketing plan, first wave of sign-ups
Week 2 to Week 10	Major marketing push, on-going budget management and collecting donations, logistics planning and contingency planning
Event Day	Who will need to be helping out - to set up - to direct people - to take photos - to put it all on social media - to collect outstanding money - to fetch snacks and keep morale up?

Once you've got these written out, look at how much time each one will take and realistically how many people it will take to do each. Don't under-estimate the time and man-power you need to find the right venue and get a critical mass of people knowing about the event through word of mouth. There is always risk in bigger events and initiatives like this, so make sure to think about the times when things could go wrong, too.

Now divide these up into work streams which make sense as cohesive roles and are the right amount of work for one person each. Plan 1-4 hours per week for those you're del-egating to. Use your discretion and give more to the people who you trust and less to those who are new to the team or to fundraising so will progress more slowly.

Managing a team

Whole books have been written about this alone, but the key when managing groups of volunteers is to value their contribution and be authentic in the way you work together. Speak up honestly if you agree or disagree with them, as it saves problems further down the line, but always be polite and generous with your time and patience.

When it comes to creating a harmonious team, few things are more successful than socialising together. Not only will it make it easier to get things done when you're all friendly, it will make it a great atmosphere, one everyone will want to be a part of.

Utilise the Internet

By now, you're probably outgrowing your own Twitter and Facebook to advertise your events and raise awareness about the cause. And perhaps you need more functional-ity from the internet too - to sell tickets for events, to have an official site to direct potential sponsors to: it all needs to look a bit more professional. These days, even the worst technophobe can get themselves a website, and here's how...

Website Domains
The domain is simply the website name (think google.com). You can get one for free with Blogger or WordPress but it will be in the form of 'yourwebsite.blogger.com'. You'll have to pay for one without their tag in but depending on what you're looking for, they can be as little as £3 a year. Try WHOIS.com to find which are available to buy.

Website Design
Weebly is one of the best tools I have used to create a website. It's entirely free, has a lot of good, simple layouts and all you have to do is drag and drop. You can embed videos, add pages, graphics and links without a sniff of coding. You can then link your domain name to the site you've designed yourself.

Selling Tickets
Eventbrite is the tool I recommend for this. Their website is straightforward for both sellers and buyers of tickets. Make sure you clearly link people from your website to your ticket page

Mailing Lists
So you want to keep track of one or multiple mailing lists and send out good quality mass emails. Two great free tools for this are MailChimp and GroupSpaces.

To learn more about website coding, you can take great free online courses with Codecademy. They're step by step and will give you real stand-out skills to employers too!

Presentation Skills

At some point throughout your fundraising, you'll probably have to speak to an audience. This could be presenting about yourself in the university RAG elections or presenting to a board of funders about your social enterprise. Make the most of the opportunity with the tips below:

1. Prepare
Know what you want to say but don't try to learn a specific speech: it comes across as robotic. Instead, remember your three key points - no one listening remembers more than that - and lay these out clearly at the beginning and end.

2. Play to the Audience
If you're speaking to loads of other students to get them excited about an event, be excited yourself, have some banter with them and don't take it too seriously. If you're asking the chair of the SU for funding, dress smartly and treat it like a business meeting. You'll have their respect before you say a word.

2. Anchor
Most people have a tendency to rush, mumble, avoid eye contact or all of these. Instead of letting your nerves control you, you can control them and get everyone's attention at the same time. Pause for longer than you find comfortable. Everyone will be hanging on for your next word. Speak loudly and clearly and look people in the eye so they can't help but listen to you. Now everyone in the room is anchored on to what you're saying. Practise this in advance to be confident.

3. Don't Overdo the Visuals
Whether you're using PowerPoint, Prezi (website details on page 112) or a flipchart, try not to over-use it. Graphics are only useful if what they show can't easily be explained in words. If you find yourself reading off a PowerPoint, you may as well not be there. You are the inspirational one they're here to listen to!

Go BIG or Go Home

Do a Challenge Event (Marathon)

Raising Potential: £££	Time 6 months to 1 year
Aimed at Groups & Organisations	
Cost £50 upwards	Committee: just you

Doing a big challenge event is a big undertaking, so you need to be sure you can commit to both the training schedule and to the fundraising demand. I'm using a marathon as an example, but there are hundreds of challenge events out there. Most large charities run their own but you can also get a place on one with a company who pair up with charities or you could just set out to do one yourself!

The key here is to plan your targets not only in terms of fundraising but also in terms of your training schedule. And it makes a really compelling story when the two go together. Have a look at our resources pages for links to a marathon training schedule as well as various companies who offer organised challenge events where you are also fundraising for charity,

In the same way as you'll be building up your running skills from short jogs to begin with up to half marathons in the run-up to the race, so you'll be needing to build up your fundraising events from the easy to begin with to much bigger things. If you're working as part of a team you can jump straight into the Step it Up ideas but if you're alone, I'd recommend starting with some well-executed Keep It Simple ideas.

Here is a plan as an example. Make sure to tailor this to your own strengths and the audience you'll be working with as discussed on pages 20 and 21.

Event	Audience	Expected to Raise
Cake Sale	Anyone and Everyone	£100
Collection Tins	Anyone and Everyone	£300
Valentine's Day Roses	Groups and Organisations	£200
Easter Egg Hunt	Friends and Family	£50
This Town's Got Talent	Groups and Organisations	£500
Car Boot Sale	Anyone and Everyone	£300
Supermarket Bag Pack	Anyone and Everyone	£100

Don't be afraid to return back to the same event more than once. If it's something like the cake sale, this doesn't go out of season and people will often be ready for a piece of cake, so go ahead and run it on a weekly basis if you find it's successful!

Set up a RAG Group

Raising Potential: £££	Time A year
Aimed at Groups & Organisations	
Cost FREE	Committee: 6 to 12

If you've not already noticed, RAG groups are Raising and Giving groups. They're student groups who have been bringing in money for deserving causes for decades. Some are now raising over a million pounds a year and have thousands of students involved and full-time staff in place to support the committee. However, there are loads of RAG groups which are smaller, run entirely by students and have minimal support from students' unions or the institutions they're a part of.

Whether you're at university, college or school, a big place or a small one, if there's not already a RAG group, set one up! Think through the support and go-ahead you'll need, often from the staff or the students' union. It's important that you can sell the value a RAG group will add not only to the students but to the reputation and success of your institution as a whole.

Things you might want	Convincing reasons to get it
To put the school/ university's name to your activities	You're representing them externally, getting community engagement and raising awareness of good causes as well as the work of the school/ college/university as a whole.
To have staff time to help with administration	Your activities, when done with professional support, have a positive value for the reputation, educational experience and

	(where applicable) charitable status of the institution.
To get initial funding for events (paying for transport, collection tins, etc.)	Explain your current financial position and the limited types of events you can run at present, as well as exactly how the amount you're raising for would be spent.

Remember, setting up a group is not something you can do alone: you will need other people to be interested before you even get started, so this will take some time to get plenty of people convinced from whom you can then build a structured committee. What's more, having a group in itself does not raise you a penny: it's what you do with the group that counts! So you should have a good track record of fundraising before you set up a RAG group or you may not have your priorities in the right order.

Check out RAG Conference and the National Student Fundraising Organisation (more details for both on page 112) to connect with other groups and share advice and experience, as well as a great social scene at the annual conference. However, this is only open to university RAG groups, not to schools and colleges.

Once you're set up, just remember to enjoy yourself! While I was on the RAG committee at university, I invented us a mascot, the RAG dRAGon. I drew him on a bit of paper, set him up a Facebook page and would take photos with the cut-out at RAG events. The next year, the committee made a real life-size version of him! Don't forget that whatever you're doing, you should have the time to be creative and have fun too!

Bungee Jump

Raising Potential: **£££**	Time 3 to 6 months
Aimed at Anyone and Everyone	
Cost £2,000 +	Committee: 6 to 10

If you've seen the Skills section on page 78 then you'll already have some idea of what needs to get done for a bungee jump!

Here are some of the most common downfalls (pun) and how to guard against them.

Site for the jump

Make sure you have easy access for the bungee company and that whoever owns the site has public liability insurance. This guards against injury to the public on the site. Check with the company you use what their premium for this needs to be.

Company

Make sure you know exactly what they're going to provide and what you need to have - like power access points, any requirements for the material of the floor or the distance between trees or lamp posts. Don't even contemplate running a bungee jump without a registered and fully insured company.

Registration fee and fundraising ask

It's usual practice to ask for a registration fee (let's say £20) and a fundraising ask (for example £80) from each participant. The registration fee covers the costs and is designed to be paid by the participant directly, while the fundraising (raised however they choose) is entirely a donation to charity. This is the same way charities work when they offer places in marathons, for example. However, you need to be sure that the full costs will be covered by the registration fees and you won't have to dip into any of the donations meant for charity. It is therefore crucial to know the number of sign-ups required for the registration fees and the total costs to break even. You should only undertake this challenge if you are confident you can get more sign-ups than this break-even number.

Added extras

You want to make sure people have a really great experience, so try some of these things to get the atmosphere really buzzing.

Photo booth
You can set up two booths, one for people on their way to the jump with a sign like "I'm about to take on the RAG Bungee Jump for (name your cause)" and one for when they've finished saying "I survived the RAG Bungee Jump for (name your cause)" where they'll be looking much happier! Remember to share all of these on Facebook afterwards, as well as shots of the jumps themselves, to get loads of interaction with your group online.

Audience participation
Set up a viewing platform for friends to watch from and have some music going ('Jump' inspired playlists for maximum entertainment). Many companies will be set up to have someone on loud speaker to make it more entertaining, too, so make sure to ask them to get the audience involved with things like counting down to someone's jump!

Pop-up Cafe

Raising Potential: ££	Time 2 months
Aimed at Anyone and Everyone	
Cost £100 upwards	Committee: 4 to 6

A pop-up café can take a number of forms, but the essential aspects are the same:

1 A good location with high footfall

2 Enough tables and chairs (this could be minimal if you're based in a park with lots of picnic areas, for example)

3 Lots of volunteers to supply the café (including aspects of shopping and baking which can be paid back from the profits)

4 A strong menu (whether cakes and coffee or full meals)

5 A charming atmosphere to make people feel lucky they found you when they did!

A simple way to do this is to stick to drinks (hot and cold) and a good selection of cakes. As you increase your experience and get known in your location, you might want to include lunch options, more varied drinks and snacks and even expand to dinners or brunches if you have the opportunity.

Some pop-up cafes have become sensations and use social media to keep in touch with their followers, who will travel especially to get to them! You might not get to this level of success immediately, but using social media is a great idea as you want to let as many people as possible know that you're coming along!

Sarah ran a pop-up café outside a local church in her home town during the summer:

"Running a pop-up café was an extremely rewarding and fun way to while away summer weekends, but the best part about it was that it really was a non-stressful team effort! As there are so many tasks involved, it's a great opportunity to bring together lots of people's skills sets for a common purpose. From organising rotas of volunteers to staff the cafe, to deciding on cakes (don't forget nut/gluten free ones!), to trying out different recipes to find the perfect lemonade, to taking stock checks and running to the cash and carry, to keeping a record of all the cash spent and raised, there are loads of fun tasks to delegate and keep your volunteers enthused and keen to help. If you're planning on running a pop-up over several weeks, I would recommend adding a new twist every week to keep your customers interested, for example, changing themes or having an interactive feature. Putting up a 'cake of the week' sign next to the grandest looking cake is a sure way make it sell out and also to raise the competition amongst your volunteer bakers!"

Go BIG or Go Home

Charity Ball

Raising Potential: £££	Time 6 months (1 night)
Aimed at Anyone and Everyone	
Cost £1,000 +	Committee: 10 to 12

Running a charity ball can be one of the most rewarding things to do as a student. It's social and creative and everyone is there to have fun. First you need to know how much demand there is for a ball. How a ball would be received varies hugely across universities, colleges and schools. Some schools are too cool for something so traditional, others are craving it. Some universities only have graduation balls, others have huge balls on an almost termly basis so you'd be shouting to be heard. Do enough people want a ball to make it viable? If yes, here's what you need to do:

Start by using your imagination

What do you want at your ball? A bar, a dance floor, bubbly for when people arrive, dinner possibly, entertainment, a chocolate fountain, a vodka luge, a bouncy castle, some circus rides, a casino room, a silent disco: the possibilities are endless! You might also want a theme to hold everything together. It could be a simple case of "Black Tie and Bling" or could be something more specific like "A Day at the Races" with horse-related games and summer cocktails.

Which brings me to.. write a budget! It pays to have someone really hot on the budget who can also work on the sponsorship. This is a key moment for sponsorship in kind. A local wine shop providing the booze is probably worth more than a donation by a corporate. Or a burger van coming for the evening for free - catering is sorted! Just get everything agreed well in advance and confirm again a couple of weeks before the event.

Sangita ran a charity ball at her school and says:

"The best thing I did was go really big on the theme. It was circus themed, so all the staff had faces painted like clowns, there were loads of funny mirrors, a big tent with all the entertainment and we even had a local acrobatics club and jugglers doing tricks as everyone arrived. Because we don't have a lot of events like that, people were so keen to dress up and made such a big deal of it. I think that's also why it sold so well. The tickets were quite expensive but it was really something different and something which people haven't seen before so they wanted to get involved!"

A few final pointers for on the day

1   Have an army of friends to help out with setting up and clearing up again in the wee hours.

2   Be prepared for people to show up early, people to show up late and people to have complicated stories about why they forgot their ticket - keep a list of names in case this happens.

3   If you have a bar, check online for all the legalities, have a strict policy on asking for ID, make tap water readily available and don't hesitate to stop serving anyone who might be getting themselves into trouble.

4   Always remember the venue needs to be put back to how it was when you got there.

5   Enjoy yourself! Of course you'll be busy on the night if you've organised all this, but you should also be able to trust your committee to hold the fort for an hour during the event. Let your hair down and enjoy the results of all your hard work!

Go BIG or Go Home

Organise a Conference

Raising Potential: ££	Time 6 months to 1 year
Aimed at Anyone and Everyone	
Cost £1,000 +	Committee: 6 to 10

A conference is an opportunity to bring important speakers together to debate a topic you're passionate about and to inform and inspire an audience about these issues. It usually takes the form of a number of talks, panel debates and workshops with varying levels of audience participation, but it can also include stalls, networking sessions, even films and drinks parties.

This is a lower earner than many of the Go Big or Go Home events as the overhead costs are high. However, it could raise a huge amount of awareness for a cause, brings together like-minded individuals and can bring necessary debate and clarity to an issue, so really hits the jackpot for engagement.

Running a conference requires planning to rival the London Olympics, a dedicated and organised team and a really clear vision of what you want to achieve.

Try answering the questions below. The thought process will lead you along the right lines to make your own decisions as to how you want to run it. Every conference is different so you need to make the decisions which are right for you.

What will your theme be? Or better, your vision for the conference?
e.g. Theme = Climate Change
Vision = To bring together local groups and leading experts to debate climate change mitigation in our city.

Who are your dream speakers?
Be ambitious: start with the Obamas and Bransons of your theme and have a gold, silver and bronze list of speakers to approach (but, of course, don't tell them which list they're on!)

How long will the conference be?
One evening? A day? A weekend?

What space do you want?
Will you have one big hall with long sessions or lots of smaller spaces where people can choose different talks? Will there be any non-conference activities such as a film screening in the evening or a marketplace of relevant organisations, even a networking lunch? Make sure the venue provides microphones and all sound equipment and, if necessary, a technician to run it all.

Who do you want on your committee? How many people? How do their responsibilities break down and where will you find them?
Think about interviewing people, look for people who know their stuff who you would trust with important speakers, big budgets and complex logistics. Depending on the size of the conference, up to ten people makes a good committee size. Roles change throughout the organisation process, so here is a guide to what you may be up to:

1   Recruit a Committee

2   Decide the theme and vision together

3   Decide the date, venue and duration, begin working on publicity material.

4   Half the committee are working to decide on and engage (through writing letters and emails and making phone calls) speakers, the other half are working on logistics including running orders appropriate to the speakers who say yes.

Go BIG or Go Home

5 Half the team are selling tickets, the other continue with last-minute changes to speakers, to the order and to logistics.

6 By now, people will be falling into natural roles. Design and print programmes, continue to sell tickets, continue to narrow down on-the-day logistics.

7 You'll never feel prepared enough but the date is here: Hold the conference!

What is the demand for this? How many people will pay to attend? And how much can you charge for a ticket?

You need to be sure you can at least break even, if not make a profit. You'll be paying for the venue, publicity, programmes, speaker lunch, possibly travel or accommodation, refreshments, speaker gifts (avoid speakers who charge to be there: it's for charity and they probably don't care about it enough if they're asking for a fee). Check out the Skills pages for publicising and selling tickets online.

Aside from tickets, how else can you make money?

Corporate sponsorship, charging for stands at a marketplace, a sponsored talk by an interested company, have higher priced "Professional" tickets and cheaper "Student" tickets.

Some reminders for on the day

1 Have at least 4 people doing registration as people arrive and a separate registration for the speakers.

2 Give name badges to speakers and make them really welcome.

3 Have someone in each session with a sign to hold up to the speakers when they're running out of time so you don't go on too long.

4 Make sure to take loads of photos, or even better, invite local papers along for free to take photos and write an article about your great event!

Jailbreak

Raising Potential: £££	Time 2 months
Aimed at Groups & Organisations	
Cost £200	Committee: 4 to 8

A classic in the world of student fundraising. Get as far as you can from campus in 24 hours without spending a penny. Legend has it a Durham student once sent an email to every email address he could think of for Richard Branson and landed himself a return flight to Sydney. See if you can repeat that! It's easy to organise, too, because everyone has to do the getting far away under their own steam. The fundraising element comes because everyone gets sponsored to do it - sometimes a single donation but often a rate per mile they travel: even more incentive to get far away!

Give everyone a safety briefing a couple of weeks in advance and put these measures in place:

1   Travel in pairs or threes at all times

2   Girls have to go with a boy (I know it sounds sexist but, sadly, women are still more vulnerable)

3   Give out a phone number which they can always contact for help/advice/a chat about their progress.

4   They must send a progress update every 4 hours.

5   Have someone with a car on standby in case you need to collect someone. Obviously if they're already 500 miles away, it's not much use, so also have a contingency fund for any emergency transport home.

And of course it's a competition: whoever gets furthest away or does so with most style / best story / best fancy dress gets a prize!

Run a Social Enterprise

Raising Potential: £££	Time 2 months or more
Aimed at Anyone and Everyone	
Cost £50 upwards	Committee: 1 to 10

Social enterprises are not as complicated as they sound. Effectively, it's what you've been doing all along. A social enterprise is in all regular ways a business but, as Robert Ashton, author of How to be a Social Entrepreneur, Make Money and Save the World says:

"What sets these businesses apart from others is that they are trading for social and environmental purposes. In other words they set out to make a difference as well as a profit. More usually than not, much of the profit they make is reinvested in their cause."

So a social enterprise can be as simple as this:

I want to make cakes and make money for a charity, But if I keep back some of the profit, I can make more cakes, better cakes, I could even buy a new recipe book or attend a baking course. So I sell the cakes, some profit goes to the charity, some goes to developing my cake business. If it's full-time work, and I do my research into the legalities, some of it becomes my income, too.

Alternatively, social enterprises can be specifically serving a cause through their enterprising activities:

I want to improve the care elderly people receive, especially by improving their fitness levels later into life. I speak to a council about this and they agree to pay for half of the costs and advertise for free. I start doing weekly classes of safe gentle exercise for the elderly:

it's social, too, so alleviates isolation and loneliness. The elderly people pay for half of the cost each time they come but it's easily affordable. I make a small profit and spend this on expanding the service to more local areas, I could invest in my own training around fitness for the elderly and eventually buy a minibus to help more people (and those more in need) to access the classes.

Of course, there are a huge number of positions between these two examples where you're delivering change and bringing in profit to re-invest. Starting a social enterprise is a big undertaking as a student, and you'll need support and a clear idea of how you'll be profitable.

These organisations may be able to offer you support. Their contact details can be found in the resources section.

For funding:
UnLtd
O2 Think Big
Local Authorities (if you are delivering a service to local residents, there may be funding for this)

For support:
Your University Careers Service or Business School
Student Hubs
UnLtd
Social Enterprise UK

Build a Community

Raising Potential: £	Time On-going
Aimed at Anyone and Everyone	
Cost Free	Committee: 2 to 4

Whatever your aims are from fundraising, chances are you'll reach them faster, with more engagement and more easily when you're not doing it alone. However, we're looking far past the ideas of working out which family member will help you to bake cakes. What we're looking at now is building a community of like-minded people who can help in a multitude of ways.

Could you find supporters who also care about the cause and could raise awareness of it, advertise events and even run events themselves for you? A lot of RAG groups are set up with this sort of Rep system. Often there will be one or two reps linked to each hall or for different departments on campus. If you give it a competitive edge and get the reps aiming towards a fundraising total for the year or use hall rivalries to your advantage, you could see engagement rocket!

Another important aspect of community is sharing resources. This could be physical resources, like borrowing some santa suits to put on your grotto. However, you can also share the resources of experience or of training. Think about asking some business students for an appraisal of your strategy or asking a local campaigning group with similar aims for a training session on awareness raising.

This achieves two important objectives: the first is making sure your team are learning and getting as much out of their time fundraising as they're putting in (we're all volunteers here, after all!); the second is building links with other groups which could open up opportunities in the future.

Think about what you can offer to other groups in return, too. I know this can sound more tenuous if you're asking for a particular skill, as it seems you have less to offer. The first thing you have which others may want to access is your network of contacts: whether your mailing list, Facebook page or Twitter, you're likely to have a massive captive audience by now. In addition to this, loads of people are looking for ways in which they can make a positive difference. You could be incredibly well placed to advise them on other groups who could make good use of their skills or help them with organising a fundraising event of their own.

One of the paradoxes of making a difference as a student is that most people are only around for a few years. This means you yourself are likely to only be involved in fundraising in this location and with these people for a couple of years before heading off to the next adventure. It's therefore really easy to focus your energies on upcoming events of your own and give less attention to this sort of community development, as it doesn't have an immediate payback. However, if you're looking to grow your group to be sustainable and continue to fundraise year on year, you need to invest now in these links to allow the next generation of fundraisers to profit even more.

Remember, if you are part of a committee and you'll be moving on one day, it's so important that these community links are maintained, or you've lost the work you've put in. Do all you can to introduce anyone who takes over from you to the important contacts you have in various places and you'll be setting them up for a successful future.

Organise a Challenge Event

Raising Potential: £££	Time A year
Aimed at Anyone and Everyone	
Cost From £1 to £10,000	Committee: 2 to 20

The Bungee Jump and Jail Break ideas from earlier in this section are definitely examples of challenge events, but don't be afraid to think bigger or more unusual too!

Do it yourself

Manchester RAG organise Bogle Stroll each year, which is a 55-mile walk around Greater Manchester and is now in its 54th year. It takes up to 25 hours to complete it (although they do offer an easier 26 mile route). There is an official charity partner each year, but participants are allowed to raise money for any cause they choose and must raise a minimum of £60. The event has business sponsors for funding and volunteers to help around the course and is open to anyone who wants to enter, not just students. Great work, Manchester! For more details, check out www.manchesterrag.com/bogle.

Pros: Running it all yourself means you know exactly where all the money is spent. You can decide on when, where and how the event takes place and you get all the praise for pulling it off!

Cons: It's a huge responsibility which can become a full-time job in itself to organise. International challenges especially become a minefield with things like insurance, visas, risk assessments. Look before you leap!

Organise one with a charity

Loads of charities run their own challenge events, from Race For Life to charity runners in the London Marathon.

They do loads of the hard work and you can add value by getting a group together and enabling them to fundraise, train and socialise together in advance.

Pros: You get to decide on the charity, they give you support, training packs and advice. All your fundraising goes directly to the cause (but a larger proportion than a usual donation will cover your costs of the event).

Cons: Compared to a regular donation, your fundraising will have to cover your costs of the event, too. So even though the money is going direct to the cause, they'll be spending a smaller proportion on their core work. You get no say in how the event is run.

Organise one with a company
There are a number of companies in the UK who organise challenge events for students where a part of the money you raise goes to charity. This charity donation is usually their main selling point, and it's a partnership which works out well for the charities, too, as they don't have to worry about recruiting and training you. However, it's important to keep a critical eye on this setup and ask a lot of questions about where your donation goes.

Pros: Companies can offer some really amazing challenges as they have staff dedicated entirely to organising them. You may have more say about what you want the challenge to be for your group as you're a paying customer.

Cons: The company will take a cut of the cost. In reality this is probably little more than the charity takes when they run it themselves due to the extra efficiency of the company, but all the same, you need to know what proportion actually reaches the cause.

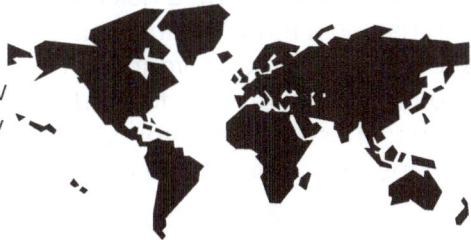

Resources

Sample Risk Assessment

As mentioned on page 31, a Risk Assessment is important for any event in order to plan ahead for any dangers and to guard yourself against any complaints afterwards. It's not as tedious as it sounds, as often it's a good check to make sure you're fully prepared.

Risk Matrix

		Likelihood of Harm		
		1 in 1000 chance	1 in 50 chance	1 in 5 chance
Severity of Harm	Small (slight bruising)	Low risk	Low risk	Medium risk
	Mid (deep cut)	Low risk	Medium risk	High risk
	Large (permanent disability)	Medium risk	High risk	High risk

This matrix gives you an identifier of levels of risk relating to the frequency of particular outcomes. You then need to plan your mitigations and policies to prevent or deal with these possible risks. Try to list everything you can possibly think of as a risk.

The next page shows a risk assessment chart which you can use as a template for your own events. This setup should work for any event you might be running, but often you can find examples for particular events by searching online. These will give you ideas of exactly what the risks are and how others have mitigated against them.

Hazard	Who is exposed?	Control measures in place	Risk level with control measure in place	Any further action required?	Description of further action, by who and by when?

Practice Budget

You can use this simple budget to keep track of how much profit you're likely to make from each event. See page 58 for a worked example.

Expenditure		Income	
Totals	£		£
Profit = Income - Expenditure			£

DIY Target Planner

Building on the guide on pages 24 - 25, you can use this target planner to plan your time to be as successful as possible.

Target Amount:	£		
Final Date:			
Time until Final Date:		x 80% =	
Target Date:			

Month	Month Target:	Shifted to suit you:	Total:
January			
February			
March			
April			
May			
June			
July			
August			
September			
October			
November			
December			
		£	

Sample Sponsorship Letter

Your contact details
Date

Dear *Mrs/Mr Somebody*

I am writing to you as part of a team of students who will be taking on *a fund-raising target and challenge event.* I am from *the local area* and am really keen for *your company/philanthropic group* to be involved in the project as I have *personal link to the group/business*.

This project is run in partnership with *school/college/university (or RAG group as appropriate)* for the benefit of a wonderful charity. *Give the name of the charity, one or two sentences on their purpose and where they work and a link to their website for more information.* I am personally very proud of this charity because of *the work they do/ my personal link/the importance of the issue they aim to alleviate*.

Explain your plans for fundraising/ the extent of the challenge event.

(For Philanthropic Groups)

Growing up/living in the area, I have benefitted from the *local events and initiatives of the group* and have been privileged to learn about the *philanthropic aims of the group*. It is for this reason that I'm approaching you with the hope you can support me to make this important donation to such an

Replace the bits in **bold italics** with your own details.

Make sure to address the letter individually. You can usually find the job title or committee position of individuals on a website.

Your personal link could be as a customer, living in the local area or knowledge of their work.

Make sure to focus on the work of the cause which is most in line with the aims of the group or company.

This is a key moment to say that the cause will get all profits and this is not to cover your own costs.

important cause.

(For companies)

I am getting in touch because I have used the **services of company name** and know it holds an important place in the local community. I am aware that the company has given support to **various initiatives** in the past. I hope that you might be interested in supporting this fundraising in exchange for marketing opportunities. There are a variety of ways you can get involved and we have a number of reciprocal arrangements to raise awareness and support for the company. **Brief explanation of two or three examples.** There are more ideas should you be interested in discussing to find something more personal to the company.

I am contactable on **email address, postal address and phone number.**

Should you wish to find more information, I am raising via **online giving website**.

Thank you so much on behalf of this great charity for your help.

Your name

Do your research: almost every company does something for corporate social responsibility which you can build on!

This could be a one-off donation for their name on your kit, sponsorship in kind with resources or anything else.

If you're sending this by post, remember the formal layout.

Follow up a week after you've sent it with a phone call to the person you've contacted.

Use your Experience on your Personal Statement or CV

Fundraising isn't just great for the cause: it teaches you loads, too. From compassion for the cause to organisation, creativity and team work, you'll become really attractive to universities and employers by doing it. Here are some suggested sentences which you can tailor to your own accomplishments.

"I raised over £500 for x cause, which taught me the importance of organisation, time management and planning in order to achieve my A Levels at the same time."

"I am particularly interested in the dissertation module of this course as I was responsible for researching and analysing possible events when working to raise funds for x cause."

"In my role at university, I coordinated a team of 8 to run a bungee jump for x cause. This experience has directly enhanced my ability to work with initiative and in a team as described on the job description."

"Having worked to fundraise for a number of causes, I have a better understanding of the societal factors which cause inequality. This is an important perspective which resonates with the subject I wish to study."

"I have worked with a number of corporate organisations to secure sponsorship funding for the project I took part in. I have the professional, interpersonal and organisational skills to build and develop these relationships, and the sponsorship grew each year I held this responsibility."

Remember:
Tailor your statements to the skills they want to see and keep it short and sweet.

What can I do with my Fundraising Experience?

Do you have a clear idea of your dream job?

I think people nearing retirement still ask themselves this and most don't have the answer yet. So if you know, then go and do it! Speak to as many people as you can in the right sector, take their advice and work hard until you make it. If you don't know, don't panic. You'll have heaps of skills under your belt by now, and it's normal to try out a number of different roles in the first few years of your career. Read on for more guidance.

Are you more interested in the causes or the experience?

If it's the experience, you should focus on roles which use similar skills (see the question below). If it's the causes, you could be best suited to a career in the third sector, working for a charity. Charities are an incredibly dynamic sector. They face challenges but they also create some of the most innovative solutions to social and environmental issues. Two great places to look are the Worthwhile Graduate Scheme, which I did straight out of university and would highly recommend, or the Charity Works Scheme. More details of both can be found in the Useful Links section (page 111). Alternatively, almost every medium to large charity has fundraising positions, many from graduate level. The website charityjob.co.uk is a great place to start.

What activities inspire you the most?

Regardless of what sector you're most interested in, it's easy to think our strengths are limited to the things we're good at. However, it's also important to think about what you enjoy doing the most, as these are strengths, too. Look for roles which allow you to do the things you have enjoyed whilst fundraising. Do you love the budgeting? Look into Finance. Do you prefer getting people to sign up to new things? Maybe Sales is for you. Or if your favourite thing is to run a perfect event, you could be made for Events Management.

Challenge Sponsorship Form

Name	Sponsorship Value	Per hour/ mile/ in total?	Contact Details

Useful Links

Amazon	www.amazon.co.uk
Amnesty International	www.amnesty.org.uk
ASOS Marketplace	https://marketplace.asos.com
Barnardo's	www.barnardos.org.uk
Blogger	www.blogger.com
Bungee Jump Company	www.bungee.co.uk/charities www.ukbungee.co.uk
Buy Fundraising Supplies	www.carefundraisingsupplies.co.uk
Casino Supplies	www.casinosupply.com
Charity Commission	www.gov.uk/government/organisations/charity-commission
CharityJob	www.charityjob.co.uk
CharityWorks Grad Scheme	www.charity-works.co.uk
Child Protection Resources	www.volunteering.org.uk/component/gpb/protectionandsafeguarding
Codecademy	www.codecademy.com
eBay	www.ebay.com
Etsy	www.etsy.com
Ethical Printing Companies	www.alocalprinter.com
EventBrite	www.eventbrite.co.uk
Food Safety Advice	www.food.gov.uk
GroupSpaces	www.groupspaces.com

Gumtree	www.gumtree.com
Lions Clubs	www.lionsclubs.org
MailChimp	www.mailchimp.com
Marathon Training Guide	www.jennyhadfield.com
MusicMagpie	www.musicmagpie.co.uk
National Student Fundraising Association	www.nasfa.org.uk
National Union of Students	www.nus.org.uk
NSPCC	www.NSPCC.org.uk
O2 Think Big	www.o2thinkbig.co.uk
Oxfam UK	www.oxfam.org.uk
Prezi	www.prezi.com
RAG Conference	www.ragconference.com
Rotary Clubs	www.rotary.org
Social Enterprise UK	www.socialenterprise.org.uk
Soroptimists	www.soroptimistinternational.org
Student Hubs	www.studenthubs.org
UnLtd	www.unltd.org.uk
Weebly	www.weebly.com
WordPress	www.wordpress.com
Worthwhile Grad Scheme	www.worthwhile.org.uk

Index

Thank you for reading!

I hope you've found this book really easy to use and helpful for your fundraising efforts! You can get more advice, ideas and resources by liking the Student Fundraising Handbook facebook page or on our website. Details of both are here:

facebook.com/StudentFundraisingHandbook

www.studentfundraisinghandbook.org

You can also use the website to learn which charities are benefitting from the sale of the book and to get in touch with the author - she'd love to hear from you!